MONASTIC WISDOM SERIES: NUMBER THIRTY-NINE

Saint Bernard's Three-Course Banquet

Humility, Charity, and Contemplation in the De Gradibus

By

Bernard Bonowitz, OCSO

Cistercian Publications
www.cistercianpublications.org

LITURGICAL PRESS
Collegeville, Minnesota
www.litpress.org

A Cistercian Publications title published by Liturgical Press

Cistercian Publications
Editorial Offices
Abbey of Gethsemani
3642 Monks Road
Trappist, Kentucky 40051
www.cistercianpublications.org

1	2	3	4	5	6	7	8	9

Library of Congress Cataloging-in-Publication Data

Bonowitz, Bernard.
  Saint Bernard's three-course banquet : humility, charity, and contemplation in the De gradibus / by Bernard Bonowitz.
      p.   cm. — (Monastic wisdom series ; no. 39)
    ISBN 978-0-87907-039-7 — ISBN 978-0-87907-767-9 (ebook)
    1. Bernard, of Clairvaux, Saint, 1090 or 91-1153. De gradibus humilitatis et superbiae. 2. Humility—Religious aspects—Christianity—Early works to 1800.   3. Pride and vanity—Early works to 1800.   4. God (Christianity)—Worship and love—Early works to 1800.   I. Title.

BV4647.H8B63 2013
241'.4—dc23   2012035561

For my five beloved sisters:
Rochelle, Marie-Geneviève,
Susan, Joan and Maureen

Contents

Editor's Foreword

Saint Bernard's justly famous work, *The Steps of Humility and Pride* (Latin: *De gradibus humilitatis et superbiæ*) is a short book consisting of a mere fifty-seven paragraphs. Even though it is the first published work of the great Cistercian abbot, and therefore a product of his youthful creativity, it nevertheless presents a challenge to the modern reader because of its tight rhetorical structure and the pithiness of its doctrine. Most contemporary readers, even those avidly desiring solid spiritual nourishment, will normally need to be initiated gradually into twelfth-century Cistercian literature. Such a fruitful twenty-first-century initiator would be one who could open up and restate Bernard's concerns in modern idiom and image, but without diluting them. That ideal person would also be an articulate disciple of Jesus who both understands the ancient Cistercian heritage intellectually and also has had long experience in personally trying to live out its truths in the interior dimension.

In my opinion, one could hardly hope for a better guide for such initiation than Bernard Bonowitz, OCSO. A convert from Judaism with a degree in classics from Columbia University, Dom Bernard was a Jesuit for nine years before entering St. Joseph's Abbey in Spencer, Massachusetts. Immediately upon professing vows, his abbot named him master of novices, a position he held for ten years and that gave him ample opportunity to share considerable gifts of mind and heart while initiating newcomers into monastic life, at the levels of both classroom teaching and spiritual direction. In 1996 he was elected superior of the monastery of Novo Mundo in Brazil, which within a very few years he shepherded into a true monastic springtime. In 2008 he became abbot of Novo Mundo, now a community attracting an impressive number of young men anxious to follow the way of Cistercian discipleship.

If this book by Dom Bernard mediates to us moderns the deep meaning and lived experience of Saint Bernard's treatise, the reader should know that the abbot of Clairvaux was himself "unpacking" for his twelfth-century audience the doctrine of the very crucial chapter 7 of Saint Benedict's sixth-century Rule for Monks, which fixes at twelve the number of dynamic "steps" or "degrees" for both humility and pride. In this chapter, which could be considered the spiritual basis of all Benedictine existence, the great monastic legislator writes in a paradoxical and even humorous mode: "If we want to reach the highest summit of humility, if we desire to attain speedily that exaltation in heaven to which we climb by the humility of this present life, then by our ascending actions we must set up that ladder on which Jacob in a dream saw 'angels descending and ascending' (Gen 28:12). Without doubt, this descent and ascent can signify only that we descend by exaltation and ascend by humility."*

In other words, progress toward God by the way of humility stands our world, as constructed by selfish interests and drives, totally on its head. This new topsy-turvy mode of existence so unsettles our lust for dominance and earthly success that at last we may begin to realize that what has seemed a triumphal way up is really a dark way down and that what feels like a downward plunging into failure and loss of self is really the royal road up to the embrace of the humble and glorious Christ. Only then may God begin to transform us interiorly according to his own truth and love, in the image and likeness of his beloved Son. By making our own the doctrine of both Saint Bernard and Saint Benedict, as made here accessible to us by Bernard Bonowitz, we can be sure we will be drinking at the purest sources of the monastic tradition, which at that depth becomes one with the Gospel itself.

---

* *The Rule of St. Benedict in English*, ed. Timothy Fry (Collegeville, MN: Liturgical Press, 1982), 7.5-7.

The title of the present book plays off paragraph 4 of Saint Bernard's treatise. There, the famous abbot, good and provident father that he is, appetizingly lays out for us a rich table laden with a "three-course banquet" that comprehensively addresses all the needs of our hungry souls. The main course of the meal is *charity*, which nourishes the hungry and gladdens the heart of those being nourished with a whole range of fragrances and flavors. But this central course must necessarily be preceded by *humility*, which opens the banquet with "the bread of suffering and the wine of compunction, which are the first foods that Truth offers beginners." The third and culminating course is *contemplation*, the fruit of wisdom, and Christ, Truth himself, invites the adept to this most solid food in these terms: "Eat, O friends, and drink, and be inebriated, my dearly beloved."* Even this brief summary of the tone and content of Saint Bernard's treatise should make it amply clear that, although it was explicitly addressed to people living in a monastery, still its deepest subject and the path it opens up before us naturally pertain to every person who, like the monastic novice, "truly seeks God."**

Saint Bernard faithfully follows the twelve-step schema used by Saint Benedict in his Rule, when the Patriarch of the West analyzes progress in humility and its opposite, the descent into pride. And Bernard Bonowitz has kept to this schema by giving us twelve conferences, to each of which he has given rather intriguing thematic titles. These conferences were originally conceived for and given by Dom Bernard to a group of Cistercian "juniors," that is, monks and nuns who had completed their novitiate but had not yet made their solemn vows. I myself was fortunate to be a part of this group and to have basked for a week in the light and warmth of Dom Bernard's unique rhetorical and spiritual gifts. I have never seen anyone so combine the mystical with the mirthful! This must, no doubt, be a talent of his Jewish heritage as evidenced, for instance, in countless Hassidic tales.

* Song 5:1, Douay-Rheims Version.
** RB 58.6.

In preparing these intensely engaging talks for publication in book form, Cistercian Publications has strived to preserve as much as possible the freshness of spontaneous oral communication. To accomplish this, we have produced an integration of the original written typescript with the recordings of the talks as actually delivered. To any listener it is obvious that this speaker is always a man of the moment, who allows his words to be elicited by the feel of the circumstances and the particular kind of audience he has before him—without, of course, forgetting his irrepressible penchant for the whimsical. For reasons of time, conferences 5 and 12 were never given orally. Since no recordings exist for these, the reader will note their more strictly literary character.

I cannot conclude this foreword without thanking two persons who, by their arduous and meticulous work, completed with almost unbelievable speediness the laborious integration of typescript and oral recordings into the one smooth text you have before you. I speak of Sisters Mary-Ellen McCormack and Edith Scholl, of Mount Saint Mary's Abbey in Wrentham, Massachusetts. They have the enduring and heartfelt gratitude of both Cistercian Publications and Dom Bernard Bonowitz and, I am quite sure, also that of every future reader of this book. Reading the appealing text they have produced is the next best thing to having actually been there.

Brother Simeon Leiva, OCSO
General Editor
Monastic Wisdom Series

Conference 1

Bernard of Clairvaux:
The Steps of Humility and Pride

Some might consider it the fundamental task of theology to reflect on the central mysteries of faith and make possible an ordered and coherent *intellectual comprehension* of them: What is Incarnation? What is Trinity? If you think of theology in that way, theology will have fulfilled its role when it succeeds in finding an adequate contemporary language that allows us to grasp more deeply the mystery of God, his life and his plan. We will have grown in understanding, an understanding that is not merely static: it nourishes the mind in its meditation and orients the person in his or her action.

Saint Thomas Aquinas is that kind of theologian, I think. There are several at Spencer* who every day after Communion make their thanksgiving by reading an article of the *Summa*. It is something I wouldn't do personally, but I can understand that it opens up a great theological vision of God approached fundamentally with the understanding, enabling us to see him more and more. As you remember, Thomas says that God is not incomprehensible; he's *infinitely comprehensible,* so that you can never come to an end of what there is to understand about God. That's a certain style of theology that many of the great theologians of the Church have fit into.

---

* Saint Joseph's Cistercian Abbey in Spencer, Massachusetts, the monastery where the author became a monk. (Ed.)

Or the fundamental task of theology might be to enable an *experience of God*, a mystical theology that pushes us beyond multiplicity and dispersion, that forces us to a direct encounter with the God who simultaneously is the Fountain of all things and yet infinitely surpasses them. Because he surpasses everything, if we want to make vital contact with him we must go beyond all things as well. Here it would be rather a Zen theology. In this case the theologian has to somehow break open your habitual ways of thinking so that you can see and touch God not just more deeply, but in a very different way; so that God is as alive and as intimate to you as you are to yourself. Among Christian authors, I think above all in this context of Meister Eckhart. He is a theologian who insists—and he does it theologically, through a rigorous and paradoxical form of argument—that the reader break through the ordinary limits of thought to arrive at the God who is to be found on the "far side." You can't understand Eckhart unless you feel your brain breaking open. That's a very creative way of looking at theology, to facilitate and even to detonate a new understanding of who God is and who we are.

For his part, Saint Bernard *does* reflect on the mysteries of faith, like Saint Thomas, and he *does* wish to bring his readers to a Song of Songs existence. (He has a beautiful phrase in the second sermon on the Song on the *indiscreta commixtio superni luminis et illuminatæ mentis* [SC 2, 2], which is the "indiscreet mixing of the light from above and the mind that is illuminated." He makes a pun on the Latin word *indiscreta*: "indiscreet" in the sense of being without any separation, and indiscreet in the sense that God is being a little bit indiscreet. He is giving us too great an access to himself.) As I said, Bernard does reflect on the mysteries of faith and he does wish to bring his readers to a Song of Songs experience. Nevertheless, I would say he is not fundamentally either a speculative theologian or a mystical theologian. He is an *existential theologian*, above all in this treatise *On Humility and Pride* we will be studying. Along with Luther (who admired Bernard tremendously; although he did not have patience with most of the Church Fathers, there were two he found tolerable: Bernard and Augustine) and Kierkegaard, for Bernard theology is basically *preaching.* It is the word of salvation that must be received with faith and, once received, must *transform the mind* of the person who accepts it, his deepest mind, and consequently alter, not only that person's understanding of reality, but also his relationship with reality.

We know that for Saint Bernard reading means something much, much more than what we mean by reading. In the first sermon on the Song he says that the monk needs to read three books of the Bible before he dies, all of them Wisdom books: Ecclesiastes, Proverbs and the Song of Songs. (Bernard by the way is odd in that he puts Proverbs first. Origen, his predecessor, had put Ecclesiastes first, and Saint Bernard inverts this order and puts Proverbs first, Ecclesiastes second, and the Song of Songs third.) In our modern sense of "reading," you could read all three of those books in an afternoon, so short are they. But when Saint Bernard says that we have to *read* those three books, he means that we have to ingest them, digest them, be whirled around the dryer by them and come out differently as a result of the experience.

So what he's hoping and what I'm hoping is that by the end of these meditations, and after reading this treatise, we will have read it in his sense of the word and not in our twenty-first-century sense of the word. Hopefully we will be different not only in our understanding of reality, but in our relationship with reality. And for Saint Bernard reality is always personal reality. As for Saint Augustine, for Bernard too there is one group of beings that is supremely interesting: *persons,* a category that includes both human and divine beings—men, women and the Persons of the Trinity. He is sometimes criticized, particularly by the Orthodox, for having an insufficient grasp of the role of nonhuman creation in a cosmic mysticism. If you read the Greek Fathers you see much more emphatically all of creation being caught up in this mystical transformation, in this divinization. For Saint Bernard what is interesting above all is human beings and divine ones, *persons;* and so reading this book of his on the *Steps of Humility and Pride* should change our relationship to three persons. First of all to ourselves, secondly to our neighbor, and finally to God. These three persons are the three great truths of existence for

Bernard: our own mystery, the mystery of the other, and the mystery of God. Bernard's book should make possible a transformed relationship to those persons.

We can be led astray sometimes by the immense literary culture of Saint Bernard, his absolute command of the Latin of his time. When I was in college I majored in classical languages and I needed to write a senior thesis. And so my professor said, "What would you like to do it on?" I said, "Saint Bernard." His reply was, "Junk." I said, "Junk!" He said, "Junk." I said, "Why junk?" He said, "The Latin is deplorable." I said, "Do you know the Latin of Saint Bernard?" He said, "I can only imagine." With my usual humility, I said, "Well, do me a favor, don't *imagine*. Read it and get back to me." I was 20 years old and telling my professor what to do. He came back a week later and he said, "I repent in dust and ashes. There is a lot of deplorable medieval Latin, but the Latin of Saint Bernard is positively beautiful." And it really is beautiful, and he is the master of masters with almost unlimited rhetorical abilities—*and* he's humorous.

He is a person who is happy to write. As you read what he has written, you can tell that, writing, he's in the midst of an activity that is highly fulfilling to him, and his happiness spreads to the reader. For these reasons, reading Saint Bernard can turn into a merely æsthetic experience, and "learning something about Saint Bernard" can become part of a respectable monastic formation program—which it should be; but it can't just be that. Saint Bernard, consummate man of letters, directs all his energy and talent to winning his readers, not, however, to winning their artistic appreciation but rather their complete adhesion to the message that he is preaching, to the *gospel* that he preaches. And what is the gospel of this little treatise, *The Steps of Humility and Pride*? It's a monastic version of Paul's affirmation from First Corinthians. There, Paul says, "The *message of the Cross* is the *wisdom of God* and the *power of God*." Translated into the language of this treatise, *humility* (the message of the cross) is *truth* (the Wisdom of God) and *life* (the power of God). That's the whole treatise in a nutshell: *humility is truth and life*. It is the only access we have to truth and life.

In other words in this treatise Saint Bernard aims at our *conversion*: our conversion from pride to humility, and, more specifically, within the monastic context, our *perseverance in humility* despite all the inward pressures that would lure us away from it. If we doubt how serious Saint Bernard is in this endeavour we should think about the final paragraphs of the treatise, when he describes the monk who has gone the whole road of pride, because the second half of the treatise is a description of the road of pride, as the first half is a description of the road of humility. The monk who has gone the whole road of pride, says Saint Bernard, is spiritually dead, so dead that the Church dare not pray for him publicly even though physically he is still alive, so dead that the only thing that remains between him and eternal loss is time. He is practically condemned eternally. Bernard is too much of a spiritual realist to propose the likelihood at this point of a reconversion to humility. It's not easy to become humble and it's not easy to become proud. To become proud takes a lot of work and a long time. Thanks be to God! Remember that for Saint Bernard this is the essential difference between us and the angels. The angels, because they are so unified spiritually, so authentic and integrated spiritually, are capable of deciding their eternal destiny in one moment, as indeed they did according to the Church's tradition. They decided either to revolt or to remain loyal to God, and that decision was irreversible. God never gave them a second chance nor would they have wanted it; they are so united within themselves that in a single instance they can pronounce their whole being in a definitive way. We are not like that; we are much more dispersed, much more cumulative, much more progressive. We cannot say in a single moment whether we are for God or not for God, and we are capable of saying both on the same day depending on how the day is going. Even within a single minute, as the case may be. So it takes us a long time, a whole lifetime, to decide which way we are going and to go there. For this state of affairs Saint Bernard says "Thanks be to God!" because, if we made the wrong decision in an instant, that would be infinitely regrettable, and if we made the right decision in an instant, that would not be reliable. So the proud monk has spent years and years and years purposely breaking

down each of the rungs of humility and making them ineffective
for himself. When the will of that person has been so doggedly set
on pride, from where is the inner impetus to humility to come?
Only from a miracle of grace, says Saint Bernard. It's a funny treatise, perhaps the funniest, but also the most serious.

We can locate this treatise within the Wisdom tradition of theology. That tradition is characterized above all by the idea of *two
ways*. Many books both in the biblical and patristic tradition look
at reality in terms of these two ways. For instance, Proverbs.
Remember Proverbs and the two ladies, Lady Wisdom and Lady
Foolishness: they are the mistresses, the guides of the two ways.
The Wisdom psalms also speak about the two ways. The Sermon
on the Mount speaks about the two ways, the narrow way and
the broad way. First Corinthians talks about the two ways, the
Letter of James likewise. The Didache talks about the two ways,
and so does the Rule of the Master. Many people are frightened
about reading the Rule of the Master. You must at least read the
Prologue and the Preface; those are wonderful documents. Even
if you don't like what he says later on, they are beautiful spiritual
documents and there is a wonderful commentary on the Our
Father in the initial passages of the Rule of the Master. This treatise of Bernard's is also a treatise on the two ways: the way of
humility and the way of pride: that is to say, life in the presence
of God (which means an ever-increasing proximity to him), or
life in the absence of God, and, because of that, an ever-widening
distance from him. We can assert that the dichotomy of wisdom/
foolishness in the Old Testament and of faith/unbelief in the
New Testament manifests itself in Bernard's treatise in the an-
tagonism between humility and pride. Wisdom, faith, humility;
foolishness, unbelief, pride. That is one way of looking at the
book and I think an authentic way.

We can also call the treatise a book of consolation and a book
of woes. Saint Bernard is very aware that on first sight humility
(*virtus qua homo verissima sui cognitione sibi ipsi vilescit*) (#2)* is

---

* The sign #, followed by a number, indicates a paragraph within *The Steps
of Humility and Pride* to which reference is being made. The Cistercian Pub-

repellent: it is very unattractive. Some of you must know what this definition of humility is all about: Humility is "that particular virtue by which a human person, by a true knowledge of himself, becomes more and more vile in his own eyes." Who is going to want that? And pride *(amor propriæ excellentiæ)* (#14) is immensely attractive, because—what is his definition of pride? Pride is "being in love with your own specialness." Who could resist that? When a Brazilian dresses up in a very snazzy way, you call that his "I've arrived! Here I am" clothes. He walks into a room and, simply by what he's wearing, he is saying, "I'm here. Let the party begin!"

That's pride. Pride is the *amor propriæ excellentiæ*, "love of one's own excellence." It is being infatuated with how wonderful you are. In your case, of course, that would be unjustified, but in *my* case there is a certain basis for it! You can see on what side of the divide I fall. So the monk who seeks to practice humility is not going to like it. It's simply not there to begin with and he's going to get tired of it quickly, even if he has the courage to give it a try. But Bernard is tireless in tracing out the consequences of these two fundamental attitudes, and he consoles the wavering monk because this book is a kind of a *viaticum:* it is food to keep you going on the journey of humility.

How does he encourage us? He says that humility is the door to all communion. If you want to live in relationship with other persons, if you don't want to end up in existential solitude and isolation, if you don't want to live in a one-person universe (which is the worst of all fates), then seek humility, because humility is the door to all communion and pride is the condition of all alienation. Pride is what distances us finally even from our own selves, but also from God and from our neighbor. For this reason, just as in the treatise *On Loving God*, one of the central questions is, What's the good of it? What is the fruit of practicing humility? *Quo fructu?* What do I get out of it?

---

lications edition of this work is Cistercian Fathers Series 13A, with an introduction by M. Basil Pennington, 1989. (Ed.)

This treatise of Bernard's is seamlessly connected with the monastic life. It is a treatise to be lived in the monastery. It is a treatise for monastics. It can illuminate and delight other readers, but I think it can only be *lived out* within the monastic context. Everything in it is monastic. It's all about the enclosure, the abbot, the brothers or the sisters and the observances, because for Bernard these are the *school of humility*. They are the setting that stimulates and sustains the laborious movement toward self-knowledge, self-knowledge which becomes like a Zion because this self-knowledge comes to have a delectable reward in the rediscovered neighbor. If you really read this book, by the end of truly *reading* it in Bernard's sense, you will love your neighbor as yourself. That's the rediscovered neighbor. And you will love him or her as yourself, not because you force yourself to, but because you have discovered that the neighbor is as lovable as yourself. That in itself would be worth the course. (I will pass the hat during the next conference . . .)

[I think that, if you didn't know up to now that I'm a Jewish convert, you must certainly know it now. There is a certain sense of humor that is particularly Jewish and that explains why I am who I am and how I am. Saint Bernard was not a Jew! However, as you probably know, there is an infinite number of Jewish males named Bernard. The reason for that, at least the one most commonly given—and I think there's something to it—is that Saint Bernard was a great preacher of the Second Crusade. There was a German Cistercian who got what he felt was an inspired idea. Why go all the way to the Holy Land to kill the infidels when we have the infidels right here in our home, namely, the Jewish population. We can kill *them*! So Saint Bernard made it a point to make a very quick trip over the border to Germany and he gave some sermons, very beautiful sermons, in defence of the Jews. He himself desired that they would come to the knowledge of Christ, but he also said "Do not touch them; they are the apple of God's eye!" He said this because of the fact that, as Saint Paul says in Romans 9, "according to the flesh the Messiah comes from them"; and so Bernard averted a pogrom. Because of this attitude and action on Bernard's part on that occasion, there has been a kind of perpetual gratitude on the part of Jews toward Saint Bernard, and it seems to be the reason why so many Jews from the twelfth century onward have had his name.]

So this self-knowledge has a double reward in the rediscovered neighbor and in the God who gives himself to be known and loved in contemplation. Just as the monastery would make no sense at all unless it created and maintained the conditions for the transformation from pride to humility, this treatise would be worse than useless unless it impelled us to set out and keep on this paschal road of transformation. I mentioned yesterday, at lunch or supper, that I have read a book about the Carthusians called *An Infinity of Little Hours*. In that book you will remember that the prior had been a Trappist. He had been a junior professed in Ireland, and the interviewer, a woman who happened to be married to an ex-Carthusian, asks him on several occasions why he changed from the Trappists to the Carthusians. He said the Trappists and the Carthusians each guarantee you one particular thing. The Trappist life is a guarantee of humility; the Carthusian life is a guarantee of continual prayer. "I wanted continual prayer," he said. It was funny because, as I read it, I realized that it isn't that I don't want continual prayer, and yet when I read that statement I felt a great joy well up within myself because what I really want is humility. I'm convinced—I think basically because of Saint Bernard and 25 years in a Trappist monastery, on account of both these things—that humility really is the way to everything we desire, especially rediscovered human nature and the God known in contemplation.

We see here the relationship that should exist between monastic living and monastic reading, when we truly read as monks. That reading is not an interruption of monastic living, of monastic ascesis, of monastic praxis. It is a "paused" and reflective continuation of the one single process. The "delight" that such reading offers in its literary beauty is meant to simultaneously refresh us and persuade us to go on. Some of you will have read Bernard's *Commentary on Psalm 90*, which he wrote for Lent, and in the introduction of that treatise he says in so many words: 'You know, boys, I really would like to cut down on the asceticism for

Lent—because Cistercian life is difficult ascetically all through the year and is even tougher in Lent—so what I would like to do would be to cut down on the fasting, on the manual labor, on the vigils, etc. But I can't, because to do that would be to diminish the crown of glory that each one of you is destined for. What can I do to make your Lent more fun? I'll give you sermons with a couple of laughs in them! I'll make Lent appealing to you by putting a spin on it, and that will make you want to fast and want to pray and want to keep vigils. That is the only thing I can do, and I think you will end up enjoying it.'

That's Saint Bernard, and I think this is true of the present treatise as well. He wants to make humility appealing and stay appealing, and so this is a trick. He might not have been Jewish but he was a trickster. Two years ago I was given the unenviable task of writing about Saint Bernard as a man of peace for a conference that was held in Latin America. Saint Bernard as a man of peace is not as easy as it seems. Saint Bernard as a preacher of crusades, Saint Bernard as the force behind the condemnation of Abelard, Saint Bernard as the person who got a number of bishops unseated from their episcopal thrones: all of this is easy. But Saint Bernard as "a man of peace"? I did a year or two of research and I think I came to some kind of answer. One little anecdote on that. Every time Saint Bernard got a bishop dethroned it was because Bernard had a Cistercian candidate waiting in the wings—in one case his own prior, because the bishopric of his own diocese was involved. Bernard felt the bishop should be a Cistercian in the diocese where Clairvaux was; he thought it would be helpful. The most famous case is where he had dethroned the Bishop of York, where Rievaulx is located. Saint Bernard wrote some really scathing letters about this man, saying for instance that this man was unworthy even to confer baptism, let alone be a bishop. But after Saint Bernard's death he was reinstated, and you know what the end of the story is: the man is now a canonized saint! Sometimes Saint Bernard could be a little too strong and a little too wrong, and it seems that this was one of the cases when it was so.

Perhaps the best way to sum up what I have been saying in this first conference is to state that this treatise of Bernard's (like much monastic theology) is a *how-to kit* and a *how-not-to kit*. The main character of the treatise is *you*. That's the most important thing: for you to identify yourself as the main character of this treatise. If you have an affective distance from the book, you really can't read it as it's intended to be. You have to fall into it and see that Saint Bernard is talking to you and the book is about you and about your eternal destiny. As a monk or a nun, *you* are identified as the central personage right from the first page. If you are a typical monastic, you probably alternate between humility and pride, sometimes ascending, sometimes descending, and Saint Bernard says most of us spend a lot of years doing that. He would like to get us to go in a specific direction, in a more definitive way. There he is a little bit like Saint John of the Cross. Saint John of the Cross has a saying that I find beautiful, profound and scary. He says that the night of the senses, which is where we are purified of sinful behaviors and attachments, should take about a year to get through, but in point of fact most people take about 20 years to get through it. Why? Because they go into the night and go out of the night and into the night and out of the night; they take it for a while and then it gets too hot and then they get out. Very interesting.

There is a parable by Kafka about salvation. I think it's in his book *The Trial*. What would salvation be? He described salvation as a boardwalk. It is a walkway, an endless corridor, and on this corridor to the left and to the right there are bars, bowling alleys, ice-cream shops, Internet hookups, etc., and the only thing that you have to do to be saved is not to go into any of those places. You simply have to keep walking straight on the boardwalk until you get to the end. At the end of the parable he says: It's so wonderful. It's so easy, it's so simple, it's so uncomplicated. Unfortunately, no one has ever done it. So, as with John of the Cross and his night of the senses, it should take one year but it takes twenty. Saint Bernard says the same thing; he says we waste too much time tiring ourselves out going up the ladder and down the ladder, up the ladder, down the ladder. Why not just go up once? He has a beautiful sermon in his collection *De Diversis*, which anticipates Saint John of the Cross by five hundred years. He says that Cistercian life is a straight way up the mountain with no curves. It is sheer verticality and you can do it. The pass is there, you simply have to keep going up, up, up, until you get to the top.

Saint Bernard thrusts you into the treatise and he makes you *live* it and not simply *read* it. For this reason you will recognize yourself readily in what he describes, especially in the second half. He wants to force you to a decision—to a decision that will stick. It is a little bit like Dickens' *Christmas Carol*. Remember that, in *A Christmas Carol*, Ebenezer Scrooge relives his whole existence in one single night, and that reliving of his whole existence enables him when he wakes up to make a permanent decision about the kind of person he wants to be. I think Saint Bernard is up to the same kind of thing. This skinny little book of 60 pages—you can read it in an afternoon—is meant to enable you to come to a decision that will last, a decision about going up the ladder of humility and trying never to go down again. So self-identification is crucial here.

As you read about the sufferings of the person moving toward humility, it is crucial that you suffer them, and that you remember your own sufferings because certainly anyone who has made it to the black scapular* has already experienced some of the sufferings of humility. When I was a Cistercian postulant and a transfer from the Jesuits, my superiors had to get in touch with Rome in order for me to be admitted to the novitiate. According to the Canon Law in force at that time, even though you were a transfer and so had already made a novitiate in your original Order, you still had to make a second novitiate in your new Order. What happened was that your vow of obedience was transferred to your abbot and away from your superior in the other congregation. The abbot of Spencer, who at the time was Dom Paschal (God rest him!), had made a mistake on the date of my entrance into the community, and so Rome responded and said it was much too early to apply for Bernard to enter into the

---

* Cistercian novices wear a white scapular, and receive the black scapular at the time of their first profession, when they become "juniors." These conferences were originally addressed to Cistercian juniors.

novitiate. They said they'd had too much experience of too many people entering and then leaving after only a week or two. They added that I needed to wait for at least six months, since they didn't do it before six months. So Dom Paschal called me aside on the feast of Saint Francis Xavier and told me this, and he added: "And so, Bernard, even though you were going to enter into the novitiate on December 8th, now you will enter on the 2nd of February." I told Dom Paschal: "Oh, that's so simple—you can just call the Generalate and explain you made a mistake with the dates." He paused and then said: "I could but I won't, and if you don't like it you don't have to stay," and off he went.

I remember that being a tremendously decisive moment for me. I stood there for ten minutes, saying to myself: "This is how it's going to be: all of my brilliant ideas, like this one about telephoning the Generalate, are all going to end up like this. Am I going to take it or am I going to leave it?" At that moment, by the grace of God, I decided I would take it. I hadn't even gotten to the white scapular at that moment, let alone the black scapular. So those of you who have made it to the black scapular have already tasted humility. As you read the treatise and as we go through these classes, it is important that you remember those moments of humility, and it's also important, as we laugh together at the absurdities of the proud monk, that you catch yourself and say, "Wait a second, that is me sliding down the greasy chute. I've done that, I've done that a lot of times."

Not by accident does Bernard twice insist that this treatise go beyond being *litteræ*—mere "letters"—to become "spirit and life." Right in the first paragraph of the body of the work he tells us that Benedict left us the steps of humility "not to be counted but to be climbed" (*non numerandos sed ascendendos proponit*) (#1). The second time occurs in the very last sentence of the text: "You will read (*legere*) these upward steps much more profoundly by climbing them in your heart than by reading them in this book" (*gradus ascensorios . . . quos ascendendo melius tu in tuo corde quam in nostro codice leges*) (#57). If you know classical literature at all you know that there are two places in the classical work that are of supreme importance: the very beginning and the very end. That was their rhetorical logic: if you wanted to really engrave something on the mind of the reader, you said it right at the beginning and repeated it right at the end. This is what Saint Bernard is doing. He's telling us these steps of humility are to be read in the heart. They are not to be counted, they are not abstract. This book is not an intellectual exercise. It is *cordial* in the original sense of the word: it is to be lived in the heart. Knowing this we should think of this week as an opportunity to be converted to humility, and, if that happens, also as an occasion to inherit the blessings that belong to the poor in spirit.

Conference 2

The Structure of the Work
and Saint Bernard's Method

We will now consider the structure of this treatise and Saint Bernard's method in approaching this whole idea of the Two Ways that I mentioned in the first conference.

In dealing with a patristic work, it is always important to pay attention to its *structure*. We know that the writings of the fathers abound in images—images which have great richness and density, and that lead us to an intuitive contact with spiritual realities. But the Fathers are *thinkers* as well as *poets*, and to arrive at a genuine comprehension of a text, we need to be able to capture the progression of thought within it. A recent example in my own case is the talks I gave at Gethsemani on Gilbert of Hoyland. I spent months doing a first reading of the text, but I would say that basically what I got was scattered insights, random intuitions. Certain images caught my attention, and certain key ideas emerged. When I read the text the second time it became very clear that there's a very strong unitive progression within the first eight sermons of Gilbert's *Commentary on the Canticle*, and that really nothing is extraneous, that everything is unified and purposeful. He decorates it tremendously and he makes a lot of diversions but he knows exactly where he's going, and if you can't see the line of his thinking and you're just getting the bouquets you're really only touching the surface of a patristic text. So my purpose in this second conference is to talk about the structure of the treatise. I think we need to know that before going into it more concretely.

The treatise clearly divides into two parts: the first part deals with humility and the second with pride. He can deal with both subjects in a single treatise, because they exist in a continuum. This morning I took my pen and went into the bathroom and held it up against the mirror to see if I was right. I'm not too good on scientific things. But I saw that is how it works. The pen is here and the pen is there and I think that's how Saint Bernard's treatise works also. There is a point of contact, and the treatise flows in two directions, out one way and back the other way. The pen is the same pen in the mirror as outside the mirror, except that it is moving away from you, instead of approaching you, and also in this particular case there is a distortion that is happening at every stage, so it's not just a mirror: it is what they call a funny mirror or a circus mirror. Try it! Make sure there is nobody else in the bathroom when you try it. I looked around a little myself before I tried it.

Pride and humility, as I've said, represent two manners of being in relation to ourselves and consequently two manners of relating to other human persons and to God. The bulk of this treatise, in both of its parts, has to do with our relationship to ourselves. Always in Saint Bernard the self is the point of departure. He's not saying that the self is the most important thing in the universe, but without knowledge of the self you can never get outside of the self. That's really the reason for self-knowledge; it is not for you to embrace yourself, it is for you to be able to transcend yourself. Without that going inward in self-knowledge you are stuck in yourself. So for Saint Bernard resolving the riddle of the self is the key to living rightly in the world of many persons and of that supreme personal reality which is God. I think this idea of Saint Bernard is one of the factors which give anthropology its essential place in Cistercian thought. The Abbot General focuses so much on anthropology, a new anthropology. I think in the classical Cistercian anthropology, particularly in Saint Bernard, the person has to fathom the mystery of his or herself and that is the way out. These two manners of existing, of being in relationship with our self and therefore in relation with others, exist in their pure or their perfect form at opposite ends of the continuum. As they come to their full realization in us they grow further and further apart from each other, but in their beginnings they are relatively close and in fact have a point of contact. There is an initial point when humility and pride are almost identical; it is before they have started to blossom, but it is very important to identify this point, to be able to see that it is there, so that you can begin to decide which way you are going to go.

Before identifying this point of contact it is worth noting that the continuum of human possibilities which in this treatise consists of the arc between humility and pride, in other Bernardine works will be described as the axis of love and fear, or charity and concupiscence. And I think that perhaps by the end of the session, we will be able to perceive more clearly how humility lines up with love and divine charity, and how pride is associated with fear and concupiscence.

What is this point of contact between humility and pride? It is interiority/exteriority. The decisive point as to whether we will make the journey of pride or humility is whether we pay attention to our own heart. That for Saint Bernard is going to be the key. Whether we live inside our heart or not! Bernard places an emphasis on interior vigilance that may surprise us, going so far as to say that we should never divert our attention from ourselves (Benedict's *habitare secum*), except when we ourselves have a genuine need for help or when another requires our assistance. Those are the only two licit motivations for going outside your own heart. The attention is to be directed toward the center of the self. Not in an egotistical way, but in the way we read in Gregory the Great that Benedict "lived with himself." That's *habitare secum*. We know that the Greek Fathers and the whole Orthodox monastic tradition talks about *nepsis*, and there is a whole school of monastic spirituality, based on the writings of the Neptic Fathers. *Nepsis* means vigilance, and vigilance means living with the attention turned toward the heart, keeping guard over the emotions of the heart. Another way of saying it is to keep the heart within the body, and instead of letting the heart go all over the place and extending to the whole universe, confining the heart, confining the thoughts to the dimensions of the self. Years ago after reading some of the Neptic Fathers I said there has to be a doctrine of *nepsis* in the Cistercian Fathers. I discovered that there is really and that it is quite strong in Saint Bernard. What he calls it most frequently is *custodia cordis*. It is the guardianship of the heart, and it is based on a key scriptural reference, Proverbs 4:23: "Keep watch always over your heart because from there flow the streams of life." So we really are a contemplative tradition with a very strong emphasis on interiority, and this ability to stay within your own heart will, as I said, be the decisive factor in whether we go on the road of pride or the road of humility. It is a first decision we make as to whether we want to climb up or down, a decision for attentiveness or nonattentiveness. It is clear that only this kind of constant attentiveness will make possible a correct reading of ourselves. Remember it is the correct reading of ourselves, which is humility, which will bring us into relationship with the neighbor and contemplative relationship with God, so it is absolutely indispensible that we learn to read ourselves as we truly are—and this reading requires a constant uninterrupted attentiveness for years and years and years. Introversion in the sense of *nepsis,* in the sense of vigilance, leads to that authentic reading which gets us beyond ourselves, whereas extroversion infallibly leads to misidentification. In the treatise *On Loving God* and the *Sermons on the Song of Songs*, extroversion leads to a subhuman reading of ourselves. If we do not know ourselves we end up behaving like animals. Remember, "If you do not know yourself, O most beautiful among women, then take your place behind the sheep and the goats." Whereas here in this treatise a misreading of ourselves leads to grandiosity and ultimately megalomania. And this is an interesting thing, and important to say from the beginning. I think for Saint Bernard you can't end up being a little proud; if you take the road of pride you are going to end up tremendously proud. In a kind of megalomania. Just as if you persist in this road of humility, you will end up making the step to the neighbor and to contemplative union with God.

Bernard uses this idea of attentiveness to self as the midpoint, the crux, from which proceed in opposite directions the ways of humility and pride. But he does not trace their development in the same way. He really doesn't give a development of humility in this treatise; instead he gives a description of what opens up to the person who perseveres in the practice of humility. That's the first half: what happens to the person who abides in humility, who is unswerving in experiencing himself or herself in their poverty without distraction or disillusion. What John of the Cross calls "dwelling at the center of your humility."

To begin with, for Saint Bernard the essential labor of humility is simply not to desist from it, not to be distracted from it. That constant attention to ourselves brings us to a deeper and deeper knowledge of who we are, especially our littleness, our poverty, our sinfulness. All the exterior progressions toward humility (the embracing of obedience, the acceptance of contradictions) and all the inner revolutions in our self-esteem (to consider oneself useless for everything, to recognize oneself as the vilest of all): all of this, both the exterior and interior side, is meant to bring us to a firm, abiding grasp of ourselves in our sinful lowliness. Recall his definition: *virtus qua homo verissima sui cognitione sibi ipsi vilescit* (#1). Once again, humility is that virtue by which a human person becomes more and more vile in a deeply true knowledge of themselves.

Bernard's only insistence is that once we find ourselves there, we stay there. This is the best advice that he can give because the temptation is going to be to run, and we will see that when he begins to talk about pride. Pride in its first impulse is an intolerance of one's own reality. We cannot bear what we know about ourselves and so we go outside ourselves. In one of his little sayings in the *Sentences*, Bernard says that dwelling in oneself until true humility has been created is like living in a house with a smoky fireplace, a leaking roof, a wife who never shuts up. Of those three things I don't know what would be the most annoying, but none of them is that appealing. The Chinese water torture or the smoke that keeps burning your eyes and gets worse and worse or a brother in the community or whoever—someone you just cannot get to keep quiet. That's what dwelling with oneself is like until humility has been attained, and that pushes us out

of ourselves because it is painful to experience that. We are looking for relief. Bernard says no; stay there. This stable contact with
oneself in one's "vileness" (the word he uses) is generative of all
the deepest and most genuine religious attitudes: compunction,
repentance and pardon, which are basic to the whole monastic
tradition. Remember in the Gospel of Luke where the apostles
preached conversion and the forgiveness of sins. Again and again
in the Gospel of Luke and in Acts that is the whole message:
conversion and forgiveness of sins. So dwelling within oneself
and refusing to be thrown out of your own house, however unpleasant it may be, generates compunction, this sorrow for the
way one is interiorly or exteriorly or both. Compunction, conversion, hunger and thirst for true justice (once one has discovered
the falsity and hypocrisy of the justice practiced up to now) lead
to compassion for the neighbor, whom we find out is just like
ourselves in everything: in sinfulness, in his struggle to be good
and his dependence on God's mercy (*Dumque sibi displicet quod
sunt . . . de iustitia ad misericordiam fugiunt*) (#18).

There is no better place to be, to use John of the Cross's phrase,
than "in the center of our humility," because it is from there that
these life giving attitudes continually flow. I read an article once
by an Orthodox nun who lives in Alaska and who took issue
with the Roman Catholic Church for calling our kind of life the
contemplative life. She did not say it was wrong, just much too
hasty. Our monastic life is a life of compunction, not a life of
contemplation. We believe that compunction leads to contemplation but you don't enter the monastery as a contemplative, and
as this nun sees it, you would not even enter in order to *become*
a contemplative. You enter that you might know yourself in your
neediness for God's mercy and that is what the monastery teaches
you. At every key moment in formation we are asked, "What do
you want?" And the answer is always "the mercy of God and of
the Order." But that really is what we want, and every time we
ask it we know it better. We know that we need it more than we
needed it before. We ask it as a postulant, we ask it as a novice,
we ask it in simple vows, we ask it in solemn vows. That's what
happens when you dwell in the center of your humility. More

and more inescapably you know that you are a sinner saved by the mercy of Christ. You want to convert out of love for him. You hunger and thirst that true justice might be accomplished in you, and the neighbor becomes the other self and the equal. Furthermore, in line with what this sister said, dwelling in one's poverty and becoming peacefully at home with the poverty of the neighbor is the condition for being lifted *above oneself* in the contemplation of God. For Saint Bernard there is no contemplation that is not preceded by this self-knowledge of our poverty, and by being at peace with the neighbor, with all the neighbors, the brethren or the sisters in their diverse forms of poverty.

When it comes to pride, however, Bernard carefully analyzes each step of the movement away from "self-possession" to alienation. Instead of being a slow process that produces its richest fruits at the end, humility that transcends itself into fraternal charity and then into divine contemplation, the evolution of pride generates loss all along the way, and first of all the loss of contact with oneself, because you no longer dwell in your own heart. The first person you lose when you go the way of pride is yourself, friendship with yourself, awareness of who you are; then you lose the brethren, then the superior and finally, God. Bernard calls these losses different forms of contempt, *contemptus*. Interestingly, he would say that pride is a certain way of despising oneself even though it includes the love of one's specialness.

Why doesn't Bernard trace the growth of humility in the same way as he does that of pride? In the first place, there is the hortatory nature of the work. Bernard's intention is to produce two attitudes in us, desire and fear. For him it is very clear that growing into humility is tough work, and he wants to reveal the tremendous blessing that awaits the person who goes the whole journey. "He who has given us the law of humility," says Bernard, "will also give the blessing of humility" *(Qui dedit legem, dabit et benedictionem, hoc est qui iussit humilitatem, perducet ad veritatem)* (#2). That is: he who has commanded humility will lead us to truth.

Bernard is just as committed to totally eliminating the option for pride on the part of any monastic. In the beginning, pride can look a little bit neutral or at worst frivolous and silly, but in the end it leads to a hellish isolation and intolerance of everything but the movements of self-will. At the end of the process the only thing the proud person tolerates is what he wants at a given moment. I remember speaking years ago to a person of the age I am now, who said with all innocence and naturalness, "I want what I want, when I want and how I want it and I don't see why life can't be that way." That would be pride. That is what life is for, life is to come toward me and fulfill every motion of my self-will, to dance to my music exactly as I play it without understanding that there might be some other reason for life existing other than to be my servant in that sense. But that's where the proud person ends up and therefore necessarily alone. How could that person have a friend, have a colleague, live in communion?

Humility also does not need too involved a treatment because it is fundamentally simple. It is progressive (*vilescit*, grammatically an "inchoative" verb), but it is always the same attitude that is growing, this closeness to oneself in one's poverty. It is less and less concerned in an egoistic way with its "personal surroundings," how others treat me, what others think of me, what life does to me. It would be interesting to ask how much of our mental time we waste with those questions: how others treat me, what others think of me, what life does to me. Humility becomes freer and freer from that inner buzzing; it simply clings to its own truth. It is very spare. It is almost contentless. Because that knowledge of oneself and one's poverty is not a raking over of details, it is not a recollection of particular sins. It is sitting in the center and knowing I am a sinner for whom Christ died and whose death for me is indispensable. For this reason, it does not require an extensive "biography."

As I mentioned in the first conference, the treatise has one character: you the monk; you the nun (Kierkegaard's "that individual"). It assumes that you are somewhere within the world of humility, but perhaps not absolutely committed to it. Bernard wants to show what happens when a monk abandons the path of humility, when he turns back on the road he has started. It is important to see that this treatise is not about two people entering the monastic life where one chooses humility and one chooses pride. It is about one single person. It is the story of one monk, every monk, every nun seeking to live humility, and what will happen to him or her if they are faithful to grace or unfaithful to grace. The second half of the book is not simply an alternative version of monastic life. It is a tale of *destruction*, because it manifests the story of a formerly decent monk annihilating everything he had been previously attaining. This second part of the treatise or the ladder, the steps of pride, is the story of a person who had begun well and for some reason was unable to continue. It is not the story of a proud preconversion life for someone who has never known the monastic charism. It is the story of a proud postconversion (or anticonversion) life for someone who had given himself to his vocation and now freely unmakes it, step by step. Because of that it really is a horror story. It is the story of someone who was on the way to union with God and the brethren and veered away from it and is now going haywire, as we say. In the case of the "worldling," the preconvert, someone who has not yet come to experience the truth of himself in any significant degree, there is something comparatively "innocent" in his living outside the fear of God and its consequences. "Innocent" because that person has not had a spiritual awakening. But that is not the subject of this treatise. The subject of this treatise is the anticonvert, someone who is really "sinning against the truth," unravelling all the truth of self that he has been given, and constantly choosing falsehood, time and again. It is this one person in his or her two possibilities that interests Saint Bernard.

Saint Bernard says that in a certain manner the two ways are coextensive. If you line up the steps of humility from the Rule with Bernard's steps of pride, you see that they cover the same territory: the twelfth step of humility corresponds to the first step of pride, the eleventh step of humility to the second step of pride, and so on. Thus in setting forth in detail the way of pride, Bernard is likewise showing the pretentiousness and unreality that the monk who takes the way of humility is being delivered from. Let me try to say that again. When we read the second part of the treatise, the steps of pride, we should feel a tremendous gratitude in seeing where we have come from. In a certain sense we have been there, and humility is what liberates us from that, and so when we read this second half of the treatise we see what God has freed us from. In the first half of the treatise we glimpsed where we are going, in the second half we look back on where we have come from.

Here is an example. I have a junior professed, very lovable. He was a very unlikely candidate: he lived in the world of sex, drugs and rock-and-roll before coming to the monastery, and most of our Brazilian monks don't come from that background. He is very introverted and very profound also. When he was a postulant he was very closed and usually our conversations were about papal documents when we had spiritual direction. We spoke about papal documents because they were safe, a safe area. I don't think he had the least interest in papal documents. I have little. Not because I don't believe what they say but it is a literary form that is soporific for me. I think his interest was even less. Yet every week he would read another papal document so that we had something to talk about in spiritual direction. Then after we had spoken about the papal document "the rest was silence" as they say at the end of Hamlet. We usually did spiritual direction walking. One day we were walking back to the monastery. We still had twenty or twenty-five minutes of walk before we got back, and at a certain point I said to him after ten minutes of silence, "What are you thinking?" "You know, I do not always have to be talking during spiritual direction. Once in a while it would be nice to be able to have some contemplative silence, don't you think?" I said, "Yes, you are right." So that was it, we were silent. We got back and that was it. Just a couple of months ago he became tremendously open and affectionate, and papal documents had not been mentioned for two years. So I said: the time has come. I said, "Brother, do you remember that conversation when I said, 'What are you thinking?' and you said, 'You know we don't have to be talking all the time.'?" He said, "I said that?" I said, "You said that." He said, "Was I arrogant?" I said, "A little bit." He said, "I'm sorry." "Long forgiven." I think it is true that when we look upon the steps of pride in a sense we are looking upon our past. My junior is not unique in that; all of those things are there in us in some way or other. Looking back on it we experience these past attitudes with a rueful humor and distaste.

It may be that these two roads are identical in the distance they cover; they are absolutely different in the way they are travelled, the dispositions they elicit. When we move along the road of pride that movement is characterized by *ever-diminished freedom to choose, ever greater reactivity and instinctive behaviors and ever less reflexive awareness of what one is doing.* Let me comment on that a little bit. If we move along the road of pride we really have less and less control. We are deciding less and less what we are doing. Spiritual maturity consists in one sense in a life that is perpetual decision making. We know the centrality of the *liberum arbitrium,* the free will, for Saint Bernard, and his assertion that we can never get totally away from that. And what is *liberum arbitrium* for him? It means that every human action consists of a reflection and a choice. As human beings we cannot live except by reflecting and choosing. The proud person, without losing that structure, which is indestructible, and which sometimes Saint Bernard says makes up the image of God in us—without losing that structure that all of our actions are made up of reflection and decision—more and more comes under the pressure of other factors in this process. Let's take any addictive behavior. I'm not necessarily talking about pride, although we will see that pride has a certain addictive quality to it. Whatever it is that you may have an addiction to, whether in thought, word or deed, if you continue to do that, Saint Bernard says, you are always using your *liberum arbitrium,* you are always freely reflecting and freely choosing—but the freedom is gradually diminished. It is very interesting that the Catholic position has never let that go. You know that there was a great controversy in the sixteenth century between Luther and Erasmus. Luther wrote a book on the bondage of the will and Erasmus on the freedom of the will. And the Catholic viewpoint as presented by Erasmus is that a human being, as long as he or she is human, cannot be reduced below this level. You would have to reach in there and radically remove their humanity for their acts not to be the fruit of thinking and willing. These cannot be

rooted out of a person. But they can become lessened and ob-
scured and subject to a great amount of unfreedom. The fundamental freedom persists, but the degree of it is much less. Those
who travel along the road of pride find that their decisions are
characterized by an ever diminished freedom which corresponds
to an ever greater reactivity and an ever greater propensity to
instinctive behaviors. And they are less aware of what they are
doing. If you take it in a community setting, the person that is
always barking at his brothers or sisters, or the person who is
always speaking badly of a community, or the person who is not
cooperating with the superior—those things come to assume a
quasi necessity. That is what pride does: it catches you and it
programs you. Theoretically you do not have to behave that way
but practically you do, and you *do* behave that way. Pride is a
"fall" with a momentum of its own, and after a certain point of
insertion in it, at the moment when it becomes a basic conviction
of the person (step 6: *arrogantia*), the fall becomes almost inevitable. For this reason, in treating of the latter steps, Bernard says
several times that the proud monk will certainly continue his
hurtling descent "unless there is a divine intervention."

We will see later on that for Saint Bernard, step 7, to know
myself as the least of all, is the key step in the ladder of humility.
In the ladder of pride, step 6, the corresponding step, is *arrogantia*:
to believe that I always know best. What I think, what I believe
in, what I want, what I decide—because it comes from me, it is
the best. Saint Bernard says that once that point has been reached,
pride sets up its habitation in the heart in a semi-permanent way,
and from then on there is a tremendous momentum toward more
and more pride.

Interestingly, we are very used to Saint Bernard talking about
the *voluntas propria*, the self will, but he says there is something
worse than self will. Do you know what it is? Saint Bernard says
that much worse than self will is *arbitrium proprium*, the idea that
what I think is right because I think it. My reflection is automatically confirmed, corroborated and justified because it came from
my head. This is not such a rare disease as it may appear to
be—any community dialog will suffice to convince us of that. As

monks and nuns, not only are we to come to a common will but we are meant to come to a common mind, an *arbitrium commune*. *Arbitrium proprium* is the opposite of *arbitrium commune*. Where *arbitrium commune* exists, the process of reflection is open to what other people think, to how other people are inspired to see the situation. What each person brings to this process of communal reflection is his or her *liberum arbitrium*.

The road of pride is characterized by an ever diminished freedom to make true choices, an ever greater reactivity. Behaviors become more instinctive. On a trip outside the monastery, I recently witnessed an argument between two people. They were already angry with each other. Then one asked to see the newspaper, and the other person passed the newspaper to him in a way which said, "You're a jerk." The first person found the nearest object at hand which was a plastic cup and threw it on the floor. All of that is unfreedom; in both of those cases, the shoving of the newspaper and the throwing of the cup, what predominated was *voluntas propria* and *arbitrium proprium*. Nobody stood with a gun to that person's head and said, "Shove that paper," and nobody came at the second person with a knife and said, "Throw that cup." No, it was a decision in freedom, but the freedom was conditioned by the anger, the self inflation, the tendency to be irritated, the tendency to think oneself better than the other person—because to shove a paper like that is an indication of despising someone. That is how pride functions: both of those persons decided what they wanted to do—but what kind of a free decision was it? It was a free decision philosophically because it was taken by the individual but it was so affected by the passions, and particularly by pride, that it seems a minimalist version of *liberum arbitrium*. Pride is always leaning to that minimalist version.

As the person loses his freedom to resist the impetus of pride, he passes from actions to "stratagems": instead of attending to the voice of reason, he abandons himself to whatever force is dominating him at the moment. Pride dehumanizes a person, making him veer between the demonic and the bestial. We will see later on in two conferences, God willing, that there are two icons at the very core of this book, one of the father of humility and one of the father of pride. There is a wonderful mediation on Christ "Source of all Humility" and there is a wonderful meditation on Lucifer "Source of all Pride." Really, for Saint Bernard those are the two directions you are going toward. You are going to Christification or you are heading toward becoming like a demon.

That is how our movement along the road of pride is characterized. Progress on the road of humility on the other hand is characterized by *liberty, consciousness* and *effort*. It is a painful experience that leads us through repeated "deflations." But it is informed by an increasing authenticity, an increasing spiritual realism, and by a reiterated choice to persevere in the experience of humility until the end. So in the humble person, in his or her actions, the *liberum arbitrium* would always be increasing. As the distorting factors diminish, the person in each one of his or her actions would be asking, "Is this God's will?" "Is this according to the monastic charism?" "Is this true to my nature as a baptized Christian and as a human being?" It does not mean that all those things have to be explicit in every decision. It means that those are the formative factors in every decision. We are meant to reach a point where even the simplest decisions don't just happen, because nothing just happens for the humble person. There is such an augmentation of freedom and reflectiveness that there is a full living out of free will in each of these moments. I will give you an example in my own life. This year, the feast of the Annunciation was a bad day for me. Not morally or spiritually but emotionally. It was shortly before my setting off on this trip and I had a lot of work to do. I saw novices the whole morning and I met with the cellarer in the beginning of the afternoon and met with the subprior in the middle of the afternoon, then we had a community dialog about buying a new car at the end of the afternoon which I didn't think went well. So at a certain moment I said, "This has been one tough day." Being who we are we know how to lighten things up for ourselves. There is a person in the community who is particularly humorous and delightful and for me, being with him for five minutes puts me in a good mood, so I said to myself, "After Vespers I am going to call Brother X to talk to him and then I will feel better." Immediately it was clear that was not the way to go. When you have a day like that you put it in Christ's hands, you go to Vespers, you pray, you go to supper, you do *lectio*, you go to bed and the next day is better. That was very clear to me, so what did I do? I called the person for a talk. Five years ago I would have called the person without the least thought that I was looking for some consolation, I wouldn't have even been aware I was looking for consolation. My mind would have automatically produced a reason why I needed to speak to that brother at that moment. Thanks to the monastic life I knew the whole thing was a sham. I wasn't good enough to be faithful to it, but the reflectivity and the awareness and the possibility to choose were there. That is the beauty of humility. Even though sometimes you choose wrongly, the context is very different: it is a context of liberty, consciousness and effort. In my case what failed was the effort. It would have been simple enough to say, "Let it go Bernard; it was a bad day. Out of the eight billion people in the world probably four billion had a day just as bad as yours or even worse." At that given moment I didn't take that choice.

For the humble person the basis of this choice is not pleasure or personal advantage or even, ultimately, self-discovery. The basis of the choice is to live in a world centered in and on Christ, who is the Truth, and in every instance and in fidelity to him to discover and accept the place that truly belongs to us. We might say that movement along the road of humility is openness to hearing the Master of the feast of life say to us, "Friend, go down lower."

Conference 3

Why Humility?
Bernard, the Bible, and Cassian

Why should we wish to be humble? We can reply with Saint Bernard that humility is self-identification; it is to be inside our own skin, to grasp our truth. But what *is* our truth? As human persons, who *are* we? Saint Bernard indeed says that "humility is the virtue by which we come to a very true knowledge of ourselves in our vileness," a knowledge which turns us humbler and humbler and humbler. But that's not his only definition of humility in this treatise. As you know, one of the ways of looking at the treatise is in terms of the three truths. The truth of ourselves, the truth about our neighbor and the truth of God. Humility is truth, but truth isn't always humbling in the sense of knowing yourself to be vile. What then is the truth of human personhood? To that question there are two interlocking answers. Better yet, the real answer to the question is the two answers fused together. The problem arises when we fail to perceive the two answers and to unite them.

These two answers are two self-portraits of the human person, the human person regarded from two angles. Both are typical of Saint Bernard. The first answer that we may be more familiar with if we have studied the *Sermons on the Song of Songs* is that for Saint Bernard we are made in the image and likeness of God. What affirmation of Bernard is more important or more frequently cited than the one where he asserts that we are created according to the image and likeness (*secundum imaginem et similitudinem*)? This means we are spiritual creatures, self-determining, capable of knowledge and love, essentially simple and immortal, the vice-regents of the entire creation. All of that goes into the definition of being the image and likeness of God. We are spiritual creatures; above all we are capable of knowing and loving. We are essentially simple, we are not something that you assemble; in our essence we are a simple reality. We are a spiritual soul embodied, oriented toward God. We are immortal. We will never die in our inmost self and it has been given to us to govern the whole creation in the name of God. We are appointed governors of the universe. God made us that way when he created us.

The second answer is that we are pure dependence. Along with every other creature, we are simply receptivity, capacity. That's no worse than the first. The first is wonderful and the second is wonderful too. We are pure receptivity, capacity. We are what God wishes to make of us and in our human case he has chosen to make us unlimited capacity, so capacious that he himself can fit into us without having to squeeze. His whole self fits into us; we are *capax Dei*. Saint Augustine invented that term, basing himself on the tradition, and it has continued up until today.

I spoke about this in Angola. On my visit I said, "*Capax Dei* means that everything that God is actively and dynamically, we are receptively and passively. We have been made in such a way that that's what it is to be an image: the entirety of who God is from the giving end we are from the receiving end." And at that moment the oldest brother in the community who seemed to be asleep got up and began to dance, he was so delighted with that. I think that's the best reaction I've ever seen! And it is true, there is no contradiction between these two answers, they fit together perfectly; the human person as spiritually self-determining, capable of knowledge and love, etc., and the second answer, unlimited receptivity and capacity. When united they teach us that our identity is fundamentally *relational*. We neither exist nor have our definition in isolation from God; that's what it is to be an image. Think about the mirror again. If you take away the original there is nothing in the mirror; the image only shows itself and comes to be because it reflects something that is placed before it. Take away the archetype (not in the psychological sense but in the philosophical sense) and there is no image, and the image has absolutely no characteristic different from that which it images. That's what it is to be image and that's who we are. So we neither exist nor have a definition except in relationship with God. It is in our ongoing connectedness with God that our capacity, our potentiality, takes on shape and we emerge in our corporeality, spirituality and liberty.

According to Saint Bernard, both in this treatise and his treatise *On Loving God*, which he wrote in the same year, it is possible to forget either one or both of these answers. We can forget who we are. Remember what Saint Bernard says about "if you do not know who you are." Due to a lack of *scientia* (which in this treatise he calls *veritas*), we can lose the consciousness of our spiritual nature, our dignity. Or we can lose the consciousness that this nature of ours is "of us but not from us." We can think that the image can be itself without the archetype. We think we can push the divine original away and still be what we became through coming forth from that original. For Saint Bernard this is a loss of consciousness of who we are, of our spiritual dignity and our receptivity. However, this is not a question of simply forgetting but rather what we would today call *repression*. For purposes of self-glorification, the human person decides not to know that he has an origin outside himself because this frees him of the responsibility of giving himself back to that Origin in gratitude. For some reason part of our perversity is the wish not to have to say "thank you." I remember that once Father Edward John of Spencer gave a homily in which he said "the two phrases that come most slowly and hesitantly to monastic lips are 'thank you' and 'I'm sorry,'" and I think unfortunately that is probably true. They are the two things that a child learns at the earliest of ages in Brazil and in everyplace else. If you give an apple or a cookie to a kid the mother looks at him and says, "What do you say?" "Thank you," the child answers. And when the kid steps on somebody's toes what you say is, "I'm sorry." By the way I think the world's best people at saying "I'm sorry" must be the Japanese. I went with Mother Agnes to the famous Iguazu Falls in Brazil. We stayed in a hotel and as I was coming down from my room to breakfast and came to an elevator, I saw a little Japanese boy two or three years old. In front of the elevator there was a sign which read, "Careful. Wet floor," and by mistake the kid bumped into it and it fell down. He turned to the sign that he had knocked down, bowed and said, "I'm sorry." I thought that was wonderful, apologizing to a sign! It is very hard to say "thank you" and to God you say thank you with your whole being. Because your whole being is from him. And so in order to glorify ourselves we make a decision to forget. It's a decision to forget that we have an origin outside ourselves. It frees us from the responsibility of giving ourselves back to that origin in gratitude. It is the choice of the lie over the truth. Listening to this you must realize how influenced Saint Bernard is by the first chapter of Romans. It is a very, very important chapter to him, beginning with Romans 1:20 where Saint Paul says that everybody can know the attributes of God through the contemplation of nature, especially his power and his divinity. And everybody did know him that way, but they chose not to glorify him as God; they knew there was a God, they knew God through the contemplation of creation but they made a choice, according to Romans 1:21-22, while knowing him not to give him the honor and glory and thanks that are due to him as the creator of all, and because of that, says Saint Paul, their senseless minds were darkened. It's almost uncountable the number of times Saint Bernard cites that passage, particularly the fact that we can know God and we do know God, his divinity and power, through his creatures, and that implies giving him thanksgiving and glory.

What happens when the person doesn't give glory to God? He or she continues in the possession of all his prerogatives, his glories, but regards them as *his own*. His identity is no longer relational, at least as a matter of choice, but freestanding; in his own mind at least he has succeeded in transcending the nature of creature. For Saint Bernard that old Greek notion of hubris is very important. We'll see that when he speaks about Lucifer. It means a desire to live on the level above that which is your own. It is the basic Greek word for pride. It means dissatisfaction with your identity and an attempt to bolt over it into another category, and in our case it is the desire to have no creator, to have created ourselves. The human person finds that very flattering but it's a flattery without any basis; it is what Saint Bernard calls *vana gloria*. It is an empty glory because not based on the truth. It in no way corresponds to the actual situation. Remember the wonderful vision of Saints Augustine and Monica shortly before her death at Ostia. They are sitting and having a long talk; they don't know that the next day or a few days later she's going to die and they are having a wonderful talk. Like son, like mother. She must have been a wonderfully bright lady because according to him they were having a marvelous philosophical conversation and at a certain point they both go off into silent contemplation. Augustine listens to the creatures talking and what they say, every one of them, is, "We are beautiful, but we did not make ourselves" —the humility of the creatures. It's a wonderful and complete statement: "Yes, we are beautiful, but we did not make ourselves," in such a way that they are pointing Augustine and his mother to contemplate the uncreated beauty from which they came. We have made the stupid mistake of saying we are gorgeous and it is all our own doing, but the problem is that it in no way corresponds to our situation, because we too like every other creature are beautiful but we did not make ourselves. Interestingly, as a parenthesis: the very first text we have in Latin is from a ring, I think from the fourth century BC, and in the inside of the ring there is an inscription, *Manilius me fefecit*, so even the ring is proclaiming it did not make itself. It is proclaiming the goldsmith that created it.

How can human persons recuperate their true glory, which is to experience themselves as the blessed creatures they are in and through communion with God? How do we get back to where we have wandered from? Meister Eckhart says that the journey back to the truth unfortunately takes as long as the journey away from the truth, because you have to cover the same distance. It would be nice to have a magic wand, but if you've wandered a long way from the truth, once you turn around you've got to go the same way back. Bernard says something similar when he says we have to undergo a *punishment*, and that humility is that punishment. Unfortunately he does not develop that idea in more detail; he does not explicate how this punishment functions. Attempting to interpret him on this point I myself would say the following: Humility is the experience of living out the consequences of our choice to exist in separation from God. The human person has chosen to "be himself" without dependence on God, and for a while God enables the person to live as if this were the case. That's the punishment. The punishment is simply giving the person what he asks for. The person wants to live separated from God and God says "Fine, try it and see if you like it." The person finds out that it's not so great after all.

Through the mercy of God, this experience is a progressive one, because no one could endure to undergo it immediately "full force." In this experience, the human person lives out existentially what it means to be receptivity turned away from its source. And what does it mean? At least four things. First of all it means sinfulness—a rejection of relationship with one's creator; then, it means loneliness—alienation from the One with whom we were meant to have the deepest communion; then, it means poverty—because if we turn away from our source, our infinite capacity does not arrive at being filled but merely waits without hope for fulfillment that does not come. John of the Cross, in his *Spiritual Canticle*, describes the human soul as aching caverns. If you can imagine us as being the Grand Canyon: we will do anything to be filled because unfilled capacity is tremendously painful. We were made to be plenified, every creature, and when we avert ourselves from our source that plenification does not take place and that hurts. John of the Cross says that because of that pain we try to fill the caverns with other things. But he says the whole creation in relationship to the Grand Canyon is two pebbles. So you throw in the two pebbles into the Grand Canyon and you can hear them clanking around and you say, "Wow, it's almost filled." But that's crazy. It is not almost filled but you heard the ping, ping of the two pebbles so you say, "Well I'm just probably lacking one more ice cream. I'll throw in one more ice cream and the caverns will be overflowing." So you have another ice cream; now do you feel fulfilled? No! Maybe I should have put marshmallows on top. But even if you do, you're still not satisfied because, as John of the Cross says, the whole creation is only two pebbles. It is not that any piece of the creation is two pebbles. The *whole creation* is two pebbles. Saint Bernard in his treatise *On Loving God* says, "I wish we could live for a long, long time and I wish that every one of us could be infinitely rich and powerful so that everybody could acquire the whole universe and then we would find out concretely that it doesn't satisfy us." He says the only thing that keeps us in this myth is that in fact there is nobody that does own everything. Nobody has everything and we stupidly think that if I had it all I would be satisfied. So Saint Bernard says, "You know brethren, I wish you could have it all because then you would find out that in having all you have nothing." It is just the two pebbles. So the third consequence of being turned away from our source is poverty. Because we are infinite capacity, receptivity, to say that we are *capax Dei* is not to give us an adjective; that is our definition. We are capacity, and turned away from God we are capacity denied its fulfillment. Last and worst of all, it means self disgust, horror of oneself, becoming a burden to oneself. Another verse that the Cistercian Fathers frequently quote is Job 7:2: "Why have you made me a burden to myself?" (*Quare me fecisti mihimetipsi gravem?*). That's how the human person experiences himself away from God. I'm a dead weight upon myself.

I read a number of months ago, in a literary magazine, that there was a survey made in England. Five hundred men and five hundred women were asked, "What are the five books that have most influenced you?" The women's answers were very different from the men's. The women's answers all had to do with nineteenth-century classics: Jane Austen, George Eliot, Charles Dickens—the whole Victorian world. Then came the five hundred Englishmen, professionals, all of them, doctors, lawyers, corporate executives. Do you know what their number one book was, the book that corresponded most to who they are, the book they most identified with? It was *The Stranger* by Camus. That is a book I'd never read. I started many times and right from the first page I felt queasy in the stomach. So I said, better not. But then

I said, "No, five hundred Englishmen can't be wrong." So I read it over a weekend, and it's horrible. It's horrible, horrible, horrible. It's exactly this person we're talking about. It's as if Saint Bernard wrote that book as a "watch out for what happens if you turn away from God." So I recommend all of you to read it if you haven't. Wait though until you are in a good mood. If you read it when you are not in a good place it is hard to tell where you'll end up. I said, "I've done my part. I'm not going to read any other book of Camus, that's enough."

Sinfulness, loneliness, poverty, and horror of oneself. If we accept this punishment, if we decide in humility to undergo the paradox of *living out separation from God in the presence of God*, because he is always present, if we accept living away from him in the light of divine truth, a third true answer to the question of who are we emerges. A portrait begins to take shape that is very close to the portrait offered by the psalmists: the human person is sinful, afflicted and poor, all of this by his or her own doing, but likewise repentant. From this inward state of living out our separation from God no longer as a choice but as a discipline emerges what is one of the most precious monastic virtues, compunction. And as this virtue emerges the monk clings to it as his or her only certainty and security. For, distant though he may be from God, he is penetrated by the conviction of God's reality and sovereignty. He sees from far off what he could not see close up. It's paradoxical: the human person before sinning, close to God, could not see, did not want to see God's grandeur—but now at a distance from God in the discipline of humility the person sees the greatness of God and his own littleness close up, and is touched by a painful but welcome fear of the Lord. Fear of the Lord at this moment is a present, because it's a contact. When we fear the Lord we possess him, and for Saint Bernard this is the beginning of wisdom. So frequently we hear him quote, "the fear of the Lord (*timor Domini*) is the beginning of wisdom" (Ps 110[111]:10).

Someone made a concordance, or perhaps better, did a study of Saint Bernard's use of the bible. It's correlated to the Leclercq edition of the works of Saint Bernard that came out in the mid-fifties; I'm sure all your communities have it. The concordance begins with Genesis 1:1 and using the number and pages of the volumes of the Leclercq edition it shows you every time that Saint Bernard makes a reference to Genesis 1:1, then Genesis 1:2, Genesis 1:3 and so on. It is a wonderful study instrument, and if you look to see "the fear of the Lord is the beginning of wisdom," you can keep scrolling for a long time because he never tires of quoting that verse. For anyone who is really interested in Saint Bernard the book is tremendously helpful in order to discover his biblical imagination and how it functions.

So the fear of the Lord is wisdom, and the fear of the Lord really is born through the punishment, the discipline of humility. Cassian in his Fourth Conference says there is no genuine virtue except after the birth of humility within the person. Any virtue you thought you possessed before you have plumbed the depths of humility isn't really virtue. The foundation, the ground, the soil of all virtue is humility, and the first shoot of humility is fear of the Lord.

We see here how close Bernard is to the truest desert tradition. Remember that wonderful prayer of Macarius, so unconditional, "Lord, as you know and as you will, save me." We have such a tendency to tell God how to save us, and this prayer renounces all bossiness. It is completely in his hands. "Lord as you know and as you will, save me." It is very close to the prayer of Cassian with which we begin every office, "O God, come to my assistance, Lord, make haste to help me." The monk living out his identity as apart from God, in the light of God, is someone who weeps, implores and hopes.

This arduous and painful truth of humility is the *skopos* of the monastic life. Cassian himself had used humility as a possible synonym for purity of heart in his First Conference, and Benedict makes it the standard. We know that what is *apatheia* in Evagrius is *purity of heart* in Cassian and *humility* in Saint Benedict, and is *humility*, once again, in Saint Bernard. So humility is the immediate goal of the monastic life; it is where you want to get to. It is what Christ is in the theology of Saint Augustine. I don't know if you've read the wonderful commentary of Augustine on the Gospel of Saint John. Saint Augustine knows we all want to see

God, but where is he? If you are going to go to him you have to be able to identify where he is on the map and you can't because he is pure spirit. He is on the other side of an immense ocean, the ocean of existence, the ocean of human existence, created existence, but even apart from that he is absolute spirit. Saint Augustine says in the *Confessions* it took him 25 years of hard thinking to discover what pure spirit means because we have such an innate tendency to anthropomorphize, but God is pure spirit and there is no locating him, and so he gives us a *skopos*. The Word Incarnate, Jesus in his humanity, the Word in his humanity is God made visible, is the *skopos*. If we make contact with him the *skopos* will take us to the *telos*. There is no way we can get directly to the *telos* but we can get directly to the *skopos* and the *skopos* takes us to the *telos*, as it always does. And here the *skopos* is humility. We recall that progression to the *skopos* is always purgative in nature and it always appears a labor rather than a fulfillment. Remember it is a field you have to clear of weeds; it is a military operation you have to engage in. It's a long trip to a far country on a merchant ship in order to get to those pearls you want to buy and then sell. It's labor but it's the only way to the *telos*.

If humility is adhered to perseveringly, until its full truth is tasted, then we finally get to a complete, authentic portrait of the human person. We started out with two ontological aspects of human nature: as image and likeness and as radical dependency. And now we have added the two historical, existential aspects: human nature is the loss of God through sin and human nature is the recuperation of God through repentance. That's the human person, all those four things: image and likeness, total dependency, loss of God, restoration of God. Each of these four aspects must be constantly remembered for the human person to know him or herself. In the exercise of our freedom we have gone beyond being just image and creature; we are now also sinner and repentant sinner. The recuperation of the relationship with God does not blot out the reality of our straying from God, nor do we wish it to be blotted out. Remember how Jesus to the end of time will have his wounds in his hands and feet, and that is an occasion of joy to the disciples. We until the end of our life and through all eternity will rejoice to remember that we were lost, and God came and found us in Christ. To want to forget that would be a repetition of wanting to forget that we have our origin in God. It would be the same stupid thing all over again in another key. Let's not do that. Mysteriously, therefore, the human person locates his identity more in the cycle of redemption than that of creation, in his straying and return more than in his being made. Many people say that the most important verse in the Rule of Saint Benedict is verse two of the Prologue: "That we may return to him through the labor of obedience from whom we have strayed through the sloth of disobedience." That's the whole Rule in a package; if you forget everything else you have the Rule in a nutshell. That's the Rule; it's the return, the blessed return. When a Jew abandons the practice of his faith, the belief and the observances, and he comes back he is given an honorary title, "Ba'al t'shuvah." He is called a "master of repentance." That's our doctorate as monks and nuns. That's the monastic life—to be a master of repentance. Because our whole life is to return to him through obedience from whom we have wandered by the negligence of disobedience.

I spoke about the "restoration of God" to the humbled person, but when and why does that happen? Once again, Bernard demonstrates his strong dependence on Cassian. For Cassian, there is a single task given to the monk and nun—to reach the *skopos*— and from that point on, doors automatically open that lead him to his ultimate goal. Getting to the *skopos* is like getting to an elevator. Once you're inside, it goes up by itself. Put another way, the *skopos* is the place in oneself which the monk must reach to be accessible to God's self-communication. It is the task of Christ as living, objective truth, Christ the Word of Truth and Truth in person, to bring him to that place, which Saint Bernard calls the "truth of one's own self." Once a monk has been brought to that point, he is capable of receiving the influx of God in the form of love, that is, of receiving into himself the capacity to love according to God, and of being drawn up and into the God who totally transcends him, the mystery of the Father. Because of the unity and continuity of truth, all the monk needs is to know and accept his true place in the scheme of things, and suddenly he discovers himself at home in the spiritual universe, linked to the truth of his neighbor and the truth of his Creator.

It is Christ who teaches us the truth of ourselves; it is his task in the economy of salvation. It is the Holy Spirit who teaches us the truth of our neighbor as love. The truth of the neighbor can only be grasped as love. And it is the Father who teaches us the truth about himself in contemplation

So why is it worth it to be humble? The guarantee that Bernard makes, his "sales pitch," is the following: "Only consent to drink the wine of compunction and eat the bread of repentance (the ingredients of the meal of humility) and you are absolutely sure of dining on the sweetmeats of charity and the inebriating fare of divine contemplation." This is the secret hope that accompanies the monk from the beginning of the practice of humility.

Now, about this secret hope: I don't know if you remember the ninth sermon of Saint Bernard *On the Song of Songs*. The bride is having a dialog with the angels (the angels are the friends of the bridegroom) and the bride is saying, as she's always saying, "Let him kiss me with the kiss of his mouth." That's the only thing she knows how to say. Just as the bride in Gilbert of Hoyland only knows how to say one thing, "Have you seen him whom my soul loves?" So the bride says to the angels, "Let him kiss me with the kiss of my mouth" and the angels say, "Wait a second. We made a deal. The deal was that you were not worthy of the kiss of the mouth nor the kiss of the hands. For you was reserved the kiss of the feet, which is repentance and being forgiven. Remember, you said you would be satisfied with that." "Yes, I did say that." The angels then say, "You were forgiven and that was wonderful. Remember how happy you were? And then you got a little bolder and you said, 'Can't I have the kiss of the hands?' (Remember the kiss of the hands is moral regeneration; it is not just being forgiven, it is being purified. Getting beyond all of the vices, beyond the passions, becoming truly pure in heart.) And we said, 'Okay, but don't tell anybody because everybody will be wanting it. It is just between us, right?' "

"Right." "So you got the kiss of the hand and you became morally beautiful. You overcame all your sinful tendencies and you became holy and we said to you, 'That's it,' and you said, 'I accept it—I got more than I deserve.'" "So, now what do you want?" "I want him to kiss me with the kiss of his mouth."

Saint Bernard is wonderful, it's beautiful, and it's beautiful because that's how we all are and how God wants us to be. He wants us to know him in divine contemplation and he wants that to be our secret hope. Maybe even unknown to ourselves—right from the beginning. We can't be satisfied with being forgiven. I went through a time a number of years ago where I was deeply aware, painfully aware of my own sinfulness, but very aware that the community was growing in holiness, so I said to God, "Okay, that must be it. They are all going to make it to the eternal mansions and I'm not. Well, fine." It happened that a friend of mine came down to visit me, a priest friend, and I told him that story and he said, "Bernard, let's do something right now. You go to confession." I said, "Why?" He said, "You know that is not how God is and it is not right to say that. You can't say, 'Let all of them be saved, it's okay if I'm not.' God has put indelibly in our souls the yearning for eternal union with him on the fullest level. That's a sacrifice you cannot make." As a matter of fact Saint Thomas says exactly the same thing. He says, "It is a sin to desire our neighbor's salvation more than we desire our own." Why is it a sin? First of all because our desire for our own salvation is indelible, and secondly, because our salvation glorifies God. We cannot give God greater glory than by letting him save us. So to renounce that, even out of generosity, is to commit a very great sin. The bride knew that right from the beginning, even though she was saying, "The feet, the feet, the feet." We say what we have to say to get what we want, so she was saying "the feet, the feet, the feet," but all the time she was thinking (and actually she says it right from the first sermon) "the mouth, the mouth." That's what all of us want and that's the secret hope that accompanies us right from the beginning of our journey of humility.

Conference 4

Love and Contemplation (I)

What are love and contemplation? We have an idea that they are the two supreme activities of the human person, and that in particular they represent what the monk or nun most desires. Probably we all have a definition of them in our heads, implicit or explicit. We all think that we know what love means and what contemplation means. The *desiderata* of the monk. Based on these inner definitions we attempt to put them into practice. All of us every day try to love and to pray.

If I had asked everyone here to give a definition of love and contemplation, at some point Saint Bernard would enter into the discussion. The discussion would be going on for hours, and in the middle of it Saint Bernard would lose his patience and say, "Wait a moment. Both love and contemplation are necessarily dark to the beginner. We don't have the inner eye to see them, nor to do them." Love and contemplation cannot be known or practiced in a vacuum; they have to arise out of humility. Only the humble person can love and contemplate. Humility is the condition for these activities, and it gives them their shape and their tonality. Any other love or contemplation will not be Christian action, but philosophical guesswork.

To underline his point Saint Bernard uses the Beatitudes; for him and all the Cistercian Fathers, the Beatitudes represent a map of spiritual development, and their order is by no means irrelevant. Saint Bernard was in love with developmental schemata; for him everything was evolutionary. So if you told him what many scripture scholars would say today, that all the Beatitudes are basically saying the same thing in different words, he would not be happy with that answer. It would be just as if you told him that all the intercessions of the Our Father are basically asking for the same thing. He would be horrified, because for him life is growth and progress and unfolding and movement toward a goal. Where you see this very clearly in the Cistercian Fathers is in their sermons for the feast of All Saints, because then as now, the gospel for the feast of All Saints is the Beatitudes. So if you want to see how they treat the Beatitudes look in your volumes of the Cistercian Fathers at their sermons on All Saints. You'll see that for every one of them the Beatitudes represents a ladder. (Very, very much the most philosophical of the Cistercian Fathers, at times a bit strange, but very profound, is Isaac of Stella. He has six sermons on the Beatitudes—they are number one to six in the collection of his *Sermons*.) For Saint Bernard the order is important because it represents this evolution, and for him there are three central Beatitudes which fit in very well with this treatise. There are eight Beatitudes altogether, but three of these are the hinges of the list: poverty of spirit, mercy and purity of heart.

In 1998, Mother Michael, a former Prioress from Belgium, was at the Central Commission meeting with me at Latroun. We were on the bus together going to Nazareth, it was a break day, and she said, "What is your favorite beatitude?" I said, "Blessed are the poor in spirit." "No," she said. "What do you mean, no?" She said, "No, your favorite beatitude is blessed are the pure of heart." I said, "No, Mother, my favorite beatitude is blessed are the poor in spirit." "You are a monk, and for the monk the favorite beatitude is purity of spirit. Forget what you said." I wanted to say, "Mother, I can see why you didn't choose poor of spirit." But with a grace that is rare in me I kept my mouth shut at that moment. For Saint Bernard if you want to get to mercy, which is a synonym for charity, for fraternal charity, begin with poverty of spirit. We'll see how for Bernard fraternal charity is essentially mercy. And purity of heart is a synonym for contemplation. To come to know the latter two, the disciple of Jesus must begin with the first.

The whole story begins with that keyword of the Cistercians, *affectus*. When I was giving some talks in Gethsemani Father

Chrysogonus attended some and he said "I heard you use the word *affectus* but I did not hear you give a translation of it. What was it?" I told him I did not translate it on purpose and he replied, "Very wise." It is a very difficult word to translate. It is strange, because it is so pivotal in the Cistercian vocabulary, but it is very hard to say in English exactly what it means. I will give an old-fashioned word here, and then I will develop it: "sensibility." I would define it as such. *Affectus* is the capacity to be sensitive to reality; you can be affected by what is outside you. It is vulnerability. Even grammatically it is passive. It starts out as a passive participle. It is the disposition to be touched and moved by what is in and around one. We could say in modern terms that the opposite of *affectus* would be *rigidity*: where an individual gives a hard and fast definition to himself and his environment and insists on it at all costs. Bernard's term for this rigidity is *obduritia cordis*, hardness of heart, and the biblical type of this vice is Pharaoh—remember how again and again and again he hardens his heart. Saint Bernard says that it is the worst of all vices because God cannot get to you; nothing can get to you. You have made yourself inaccessible to reality. The first time I gave these talks was in Quilvo, Chile, and at some point in the question-and-answer session one of the older sisters, who was vocation director, said, "What would be a criterion for you not to accept somebody into the community?" Probably because I was giving these talks I said exactly this, it would be *obduritia cordis*. Sometimes you're dealing with a person whom you feel has already finished their journey, in the sense that nothing is going to touch them anymore. The shell has formed, the complete version is there. There is not going to be any more growth. Nothing new is going to get in. I would say there is no reason to take that person into monastic life. So I say that for Saint Bernard it is really the most dangerous of spiritual alternatives. An *affectus* with a capacity to be moved is the best possibility.

By now we know that in Bernard's way of thinking the first person whom we should be "affected" by is we ourselves. That's a process that never ends, to taste ourselves. To know ourselves as we really *do* know ourselves, but try not to. When I was a novice

I was in the schola early on. There was someone else in the schola whose name will remain anonymous, and for some reason, which was no reason, I detested him. He was a very nice person but I couldn't stand him. And one day he was the subcantor and he intoned the psalm at None. He made a mistake and I was thrilled. I was practically doing somersaults in the stalls. "You idiot, you fool, you can't even intone a simple sixth tone psalm, anybody could do that. The dog could do that and you can't do that, you're a fool, you should never have been put in the schola. You shouldn't have come into the monastery. I don't think you should ever have been born." All of this passed through my mind. Then I got frightened and I said, "Wow, where did this come from?" So I went to speak to another novice, who was also a priest, and he said, "Well, you are probably having a bad day. Don't worry about it." I said, "I don't think I was having such a bad day." He said. "Well, we will chalk it up to the devil." "Okay." It was a relief, but I didn't feel exactly right about it so I went to the assistant novice director, who was Brother Aelred. And I told him the whole story in all its gory detail and I told him what the priest had said. He asked me, "Who do *you* think it was?" "I don't know," I said. He said, "Well who do you think it could be?" "Well, it couldn't be me." He said, "No? Why couldn't it be you?" I said, "Because I'm not that kind of person." He said, "Funny, I thought you were." We have to be affected by ourselves. First of all, that means to be affected about myself through the stimulus of another person. But we have to learn to listen to everything that our heart is saying and sometimes it is absolutely bestial or demonic, subhuman, terrible. You don't have to say yes to it, but if your heart is saying it, you have to hear it. The Abbot General once said to me, "Don't be afraid of anything that comes from yourself, it is only yourself." And I think there's a lot of wisdom to that. So the first great step of *affectus* is to allow all that is inside of ourselves to manifest itself, to declare itself, to pronounce itself. And that can only happen if we live interiorly. That's why it's so important for novices and juniors to practice solitude in silence. This being affected by oneself can only happen in a climate of solitude and silence. I'm sure that when monks talk too much it is because it's painful to discover what the heart is saying. Now Jesus was very honest about that. Remember how he said it is not what goes into the stomach that defiles a person, but what comes out of the heart. And he gave a whole list of what comes out of the heart and it's not very flattering, but very true. Those things come out of the heart. Saint Bernard in a very delicate statement says, "Let's face it, brothers, our heart is a sewer." It cannot get any stronger than that. And he says solitude and silence will first let us see it for what it is and then it will provide clean water to flow into the sewer and to purify it progressively. But the first step is to accept that this is how things are. Given the existential alienation I spoke about in the conference this morning, to be affected by ourselves will be to feel our wretchedness, our *miseria*—that great word of Saint Bernard—to feel it inescapably. And humility will be a persistent openness to this experience, painful though it is, precisely because it is recognized as true. I tell young people at Novo Mundo that a bad truth is one hundred times better than a good lie. Anything that's true is precious, however unpleasant it is. And anything that is false is worthless, however glorious it may seem. I don't know if you know that very provocative statement by Simone Weil. She loved Christ tremendously but she once wrote that if you have to choose between Christ and the truth, choose the truth, because the truth will always lead you to Christ whereas your idea of Christ may not always be the truth. So truth is worth everything; certainly for Saint Bernard. Humility is to own it, to abide in it, to "abide in my word." When I was a novice reading around in the medieval tradition I saw this whole custom of spiritual marriage: the most famous cases are those of Saint Francis who married himself to Lady Poverty, and Blessed Henry Suso in the fourteenth century, a Dominican mystic, a disciple of Eckhart, who married himself to Lady Wisdom. So with the novice director's permission I had my own nuptials, and I married myself to Lady Truth. He asked me before I went ahead with the marriage, "Are you sure you want to do it? She is one tough lady." I said, "I do." He said, "Okay, I now pronounce you man and wife." I even had a simple card with the words "Lady Truth" on it that I carried around in my habit pocket all through the novitiate just so that I would not lose contact with her. Humility is our marriage with Lady Truth. Pride, on the other hand, will do everything possible to avoid this experience. It will actually *work with all its might* to render itself insensible to vital contact with its poverty. As we will see later, the whole descending ladder of pride is a pitched battle to keep yourself from knowing your nothingness. That's what pride is after; it's running away from your experience of poverty, it's one long flight from the experience of your poverty because it is the love of one's specialness, as Saint Bernard defines it. For in its essence, pride is *amor propriae excellentiae:* a commitment to, an embrace of, one's specialness. If this embrace is tight enough nothing will bring the proud person to this first, indispensable *affectus.* To be touched by your own truth.

But why does this *affectus,* this being touched by your own poverty, lead to love, and what kind of love does it lead to? First we remember that we are constantly in connection with other persons. All other human persons are our *socii,* says Bernard, our companions, our partners, our colleagues. We all have the same nature and this nature is essentially cenobitic (Bernard believes firmly in Saint Basil's affirmation that angels and animals can live in isolation, but human beings are social in their very structure). This means that we are always looking at each other, always defining ourselves in relation to each other, always defining others in reference to ourselves. This is not sinful; it is simply the consequence of our interconnectedness in the one big Adam. Basically we are one person, each with his or her own indestructible individuality. There is only one Adam, and that is all of us, so we are all partners, members in this one great Adam. An excellent book (which, if you have not read it, I recommend you do so) is *Catholicism* by De Lubac. I think the subtitle is "The Social Nature of the Dogma." There he explains that we mistake what original sin is and what salvation is. Original Sin is not just the rupture between God and us. It's also the rupture between us human beings, and salvation is not simply reconciliation with God. It is the reconstruction of the one Adam and the one Adam is the Church. As Cyril of Jerusalem says, "God created the universe in view of the Church" and the Church is the re-collection, the reassembly of all peoples in the one great Adam, whose head is Christ. So we are all partners in this enterprise of being human beings and always in relation to each other. The problem is that until we are affected by ourselves, by our poverty, until we have admitted it and tasted it, the glance at the neighbor is inevitably self-aggrandizing and other-depreciating. Whenever we look at the neighbor before we have been touched by our own poverty we always come out on top; this is just inevitable. I look, I see his faults and my virtue, her faults and my virtue, his inferiority and my superiority. The neighbor at this stage of the game is a wonderful "make me feel good" pill! I swallow him and I feel better about myself because he's worse than I am. I might do X, Y and Z but look at what he does. Look at what she does. Look at how they are. Looking at the neighbor, I see and despise his faults and I rejoice and exult that I am cut from a different cloth. Until we have passed profoundly through the first *affectus* our model for fraternal relations is the Pharisee of Luke 18, "I thank you God that I am not like other men." That's until we have tasted our poverty. We are simply delighted that God has made a single exception and everybody else is the publican.

What happens when we *are* affected? The constant glance at the neighbor shows us something hitherto unknown: that *we too are included* in the universal condemnation of our sharp eye. Saint Bernard says that the proud person, the person who has not been touched by his poverty, is always praying Psalm 115, "No one can be trusted. No one can be trusted. No one can be trusted"—in the Latin, *omnis homo mendax*, every man is false, every other person is a fake, is a liar. And that's how we feel until we have been touched by our poverty. But we don't understand, says Saint Bernard: *omnis* means *omnis*, and that means absolutely *everyone*. Brother Aelred once asked me, "What did the novitiate teach you?" I said, "It taught me to see not just what was outside of my head, but what was inside my head as well. It opened the eyes at the back of my head. So instead of just seeing from the front of my head to the outside world, I see from the back of my head to the front of my own head and from there to the outside world." And what our poverty shows us when we see what is inside our own head is that there are no exceptions. *Omnis homo mendax.*

This solidarity, this identification with the neighbor, Bernard says, brings forth from us a wave of tenderness. The misery of the other, which previously stimulated sentiments of distancing and ridicule in us, now wins our instinctive sympathy. We know how awful the other must be feeling in his poverty, because it is an experience that we have tasted to the dregs. More than that: we know what he is feeling *because we feel it with him.* As you know, the key Pauline mystical term is the preposition "cum" (with)—*commori, consepultari, concrucifigi, consurgere*—we "with-die" with Christ, we are "with-buried" with Christ, we are "with-crucified" with Christ, we are "with-risen" with Christ. When translated into better English we say, "We are crucified with Christ, we are raised with Christ." It is a very intense identification, and the same prefix functions within Bernadine charity. We go through the neighbor's experience. We suffer the neighbor's plight together with the neighbor. What has happened is that our *affectus* has been stretched to include the other. But evidently unless this *affectus* emerges in the first place through the encounter with oneself in humility, there would be nothing to stretch.

Bernard's notion of genuine fraternal love, therefore, is neither romantic nor "disinterested." It is, rather, sympathetic and compassionate. Romantic love is based on admiration and the desire to possess. When we fall in love with a beautiful woman it is not because we feel bad for her. It's because she's beautiful and we admire it and we want it for ourselves. The most wonderful study of the limits of romantic love is the book *Works of Love* by Kierkegaard. Some people describe it as the nineteenth-century *Imitation of Christ.* It is a very profound book; hard to read but well worth reading. He goes so far as to say that Christian love has only one object, which is the neighbor; it can't be exclusive. Exclusive love, whether it's for a friend or in the case of a man for a woman or of a woman for a man, is always self-aggrandizing love. It's the recognition of value and the desire to have it for oneself. And the sense that possessing that will increase me, make me greater, because now I possess this object of tremendous value.

So whereas romantic love is based on admiration and desire to possess, monastic, Christian love is founded on an irresistible urge to be with and console the other in his affliction. We know Saint Bernard was a genius. That's the presupposition of this course. I think he was able to go a step beyond Kierkegaard.

I'm not sure how many of you are familiar with this play of words of Bernard which is very rich: *amor veritatis et veritas amoris:* the love of the truth and the truth of love. Saint Bernard says that the Christian will be drawn in two directions by his love. The *amor veritatis* is not something to get rid of, and this is the love of admiration—we love things according to their value. Bernard feels this is completely valid and you can't get rid of it. You love a good person better than a bad person in this love; you love a good poem more than a mediocre poem. You love a great painting more than an awful painting, you love a person who has saved your life more than someone who hasn't saved your life, or wouldn't save your life. You love God above all things. You love here according to the truth of the object and that elicits your love. But there is a second love, he says; Christ has taught us another love. It doesn't eliminate the first love, but it is a newness in the world. It is the truth of charity, and in this case the direction is the opposite. Our love is drawn to the person who is needier rather than the person who is less needy. The person who is in tougher shape rather than the person who doesn't really need us. The person who is more alienated from God, more distorted, paralyzed rather than the person who is doing well. The poor rather than the wealthy. The sad rather than the happy-go-lucky. As monks and as Christians we are called to have both of those loves. But the novelty of the Gospel is this: that our heart should be drawn to what is weakest; and it seems to be how God works also. God has chosen the foolish of the world, the weak of the world, the poor of the world and the humble of the world. It's to be drawn lovingly to where we can help and to where we can be with those who need us most.

So what Saint Bernard is talking about here, although this term doesn't appear in this treatise, is the truth of love. That when we have been touched by our own poverty, our love is drawn spontaneously to where there is affliction. So many of the great saints of the church could not help loving those who were the most down and out in whatever way it might be. Think of a Saint Vincent de Paul or of a Mother Teresa, a Martin de Porres. It can be on whatever level. It does not have to be a financial difficulty. It can be physical, moral or spiritual poverty. It is the Christ who goes out leaving the ninety nine on the hillside and going out after the one. And this spontaneous attraction, this irresistible attraction to console the other in their affliction, only comes through tasting our own poverty according to Saint Bernard.

How do we express this love concretely? Saint Bernard says, through the fruits of the Holy Spirit. The "stretching" of the *affectus* (remember how I spoke about how the *affectus* gets stretched), the stretching that enables the neighbor to be carried in one's own heart is the transforming work of the Spirit within the humbled religious. According to medieval pharmacology, when you poured oil on the skin of an animal, it stretched. If you had a skin and you needed to make it a little bit bigger, because it didn't get as far as you wanted it to get, you poured some oil on it, you rubbed in the oil and the skin became more flexible and enlarged. Saint Bernard says, "Well, that's it. That's the Holy Spirit." He is poured onto the skin of our hearts, and God kneads him into the skin of our hearts, and our *affectus* is stretched and includes not only ourselves but the neighbor. There is a passage in one of the prophetic books about having a blanket too narrow for two. Only one person can fit under the blanket. "Don't ask me to cover you with my blanket; my blanket is only big enough for one." And Saint Bernard says that if we have passed through the humiliation of this first *affectus* our blanket gets bigger, so there is always room for the second person, whoever the neighbor may be. As a result of this we relate to the neighbor in a "spiritual" way, meaning the way of the Holy Spirit: our interaction with the neighbor is henceforth characterized by "peace, patience, kindness, long suffering and joy" (#4). Evidently he is listing the fruits of the Holy Spirit. Our love for the neighbor is *humanized divine love*, which seeks nothing for itself—nor needs to, because its delight is in the activity of loving which the monk recognizes as the capacity to communicate what he has received from the Spirit. I think it is John of Ford in one of his sermons who says to God, "Don't love me, make me love you." God says to John, "What you talking about?" And John says, "If you love me, that's nice, but that means divine love is in you and I am only the object of it. If I love you that means divine love is in me and I love you with your own divine love. That's much closer. That's more intimate. I don't want the first one—I can't be satisfied with that. Teach me to love you, because that's the fullness of the intimacy." There is something of that here in the second course of the banquet of love, where fraternal charity emerges because of one's inner poverty: the person is completely satisfied with loving, because he understands that within the active, genuine, human loving, the divine is at work. The divine subject is there loving within and through the human subject. I think that's part of what Saint Bernard was saying in that famous quote, "I love because I love. I love so that I can continue to love." *Amo quia amo; amo ut amem.* He recognizes that the act of loving is the act of being inhabited by and moved by and intersubjected by the Holy Spirit. Thus this monk, affected by the neighbor, this monk of the "enlarged heart," recognizes that he is henceforth being nourished on a diet of divine charity.

Saint Bernard says that the love of neighbor represents a second stage in the monk's single search for truth. One great lesson the monk has learned through the expansion of his *affectus* is that the search for truth requires diverse methodologies according to its object. There are different ways of seeking truth which are not interchangeable. He now perceives that up to this point he had been applying the methodology of *observation, analysis and judgment* to the study of the neighbor (*diiudicare*). All of these Saint Bernard sums up in the word *diiudicare*. I think we all do this spontaneously and maybe unfortunately. I've known you for less than thirty hours. I already have all sorts of reactions and ideas about each one of you, based on your appearance, based on what you said in chapter last night, based on your sense of humor, based on your gestures and all of that. That's observation, analysis and judgment, and this method invariably leads to a negative evaluation (*omnis homo mendax*). If I look long enough at you that way I'm going to see the warts and all. That's what happens when we look at the neighbor that way. It would be nice to say that the more I look, the more I find to be delighted with, but we know that's not true. Remember how we felt about the community the first week when they were all saints, and how different it was six weeks later, six months later, six years later. If what you use with the neighbor is the methodology of observation, analysis, and judgment it is going to come out negative. But now the monk perceives that this manner of pursuing truth is proper for "self-study." God asks us to apply that to ourselves or to let him apply it to us. He asks us to be open to be seen in the pitiless—and then afterward merciful—light of truth. That's how we should be with regards to our own self. I don't know if I quoted here the wonderful passage from *The Brothers Karamazov*. (It sounds as if I have twenty copies in my briefcase and I'll be selling them afterward.) But we know that in the nineteenth century there was a revival of the tradition of the holy man, the staretz, and that people would travel hundreds of miles on foot to have a five-minute conversation with one of them. There is a scene very close to the beginning of the book where people are flooding in upon the staretz Zosima to talk to him, and there is a society lady, who really only wants to speak with him because it is fashionable to talk to an elder. Her spirituality is shallow, but when she gets back to Saint Petersburg she wants to say she spoke to the elder, because he's the one to talk to. It is like a Hollywood actor talking to a swami. So she has to speak with the elder, and the elder speaks kindly to her, and finally she says what she knows she should say, "Elder, give me a word." We all know that "give me a word of life." The elder tells her, "Never lie, and above all, never lie to yourself." This is a teaching of humility. If we do not lie to ourselves we submit to letting ourselves be seen by, analyzed by, judged by and forgiven by Christ This is right in relationship to ourselves. Never lie to yourself. But it's not the way to make the truth of the neighbor become accessible. The neighbor can never be known that way. The neighbor's inner door will never swing open to such observation, however sharp, perceptive and persevering it may be. Saint Bernard says that to know the neighbor in his/her truth, the only genuine instrument is compassion for the neighbor in his sufferings. He says, "We seek for the truth in the neighbor by having compassion on his suffering." *(Inquirimus veritatem in proximis, eorum malis compatiendo)* (#6). If you want to find out what the truth of your neighbor is, have compassion on his suffering; this is the only way you can touch the truth of the neighbor. The more we are "affected" by him/her the more we have compassion for their sufferings, the more we will know them. It is the old adage of Gregory the Great: *Amor ipse notitia est* (Hom Ev 2.27). Love is knowledge. You will know the neighbor to the extent that you truly love him or her in this compassionate way.

Reflecting on Saint Bernard's treatment of the Pharisee and the publican (#17), we see that the Pharisee's problem is that he inverted his methodologies. He regarded himself with benevolent sympathy. So benevolent that he failed to perceive who he was and how he was, and looked on the publican with the analytical eye of "justice." The publican, on the other hand, at least got the first step right: looking at himself unswervingly in the light of truth, he identified himself as a sinner in need of mercy. "Have mercy on me a sinner." He could go home justified—hopefully to return to the Temple the next day to pass from *affectus* to *conaffectus*. Hopefully the next day when he returned to the temple he prayed, "Have mercy on us, sinners." That's the second degree of truth, love for the neighbor in compassion.

Christian love, then, is a communion in poverty. It does not consider the neighbor's qualities, talents, abilities, nor his faults, but his *plight*. It brings to the neighbor Christian love with whatever riches of the Spirit it may possess, because the expansion of the *affectus* has put an end to spiritual individualism, to discrimination between "you" and "me" and a resultant protectiveness of "me" against "you." The expanded *affectus* turns into a reality—makes a reality—what Paul preaches: to be *one* in Christ Jesus. The person who lives the second degree of truth, which is fraternal charity, lives this way: You-I poor and needy, not You and I; it is closer than that. You-I, poor and needy, You-I capable of aiding one another in Christ, You-I looking up to God to seek all things from him and simply to *see* him. If you know Baldwin of Ford's *Treatise on the Cenobitic Life*, which is very popular these days, he speaks about three communions that we have, and our first communion is a universal communion in having a human nature and being sinful and being sorrowful. Every time we sing the *Salve* we are proclaiming that communion. "To thee do we cry, poor banished children of Eve." Baldwin says that's not so bad—and it really isn't. It's the beginning of salvation when we acknowledge who we are, what our sin is, our sorrowfulness; and that makes us enter into communion with everybody. How beautiful that the *Salve* is in the plural and not in the singular. "To thee do *we* lift up our eyes, poor banished children of Eve"— all of us making our way back together into the garden which is paradise and which is monastic life.

Conference 5

Love and Contemplation (II)

Every young monk wants to start with God. Every novice comes to the monastery armed with his copy of John of the Cross. God willing, by the time he finishes his monastic race, he is content with the Rule and the Psalter.

God in his kindness usually allows the fervent novice a short time of "thinking he sees him" (or, William of Saint Thierry would put it, to see him briefly as an anticipated grace and a stimulus for future fidelity). In a short time, however, the screen goes black. What has happened?

Once again, it is a question of methodology, instruments and *affectus*. The desire to see God, Saint Bernard says, is the culmination of the search for truth. It has to be, because whereas we ourselves and our neighbor "possess" a truth, God *is* Truth: *Veritas in se ipsa*. We have seen that we search out our truth by judgment and the neighbor's by compassion. If we want to grasp God in his Truth, the methodology to be followed is contemplation: *Inquirimus veritatem in sui natura . . . contemplando*. Neither analysis nor sentiments of solidarity will make the God of mystery visible to us.

We know that and we think we have gotten around the problem by developing all kinds of techniques of contemplation. But techniques of contemplation do not bring us closer to the understanding or activity of contemplation. Contemplation begins to take place when a radical change has been effected in us by the pressure of truth.

Discovering the truth of love (*veritas amoris*) became a possibility for us when we were changed into humble persons by the force truth exercises on us. For years we tried as Christians and monastics to love our brothers and sisters, but we failed because we tried to learn the neighbor's truth as the persons we were. Only when truth-as-it-has-to-do-with-us altered us, did love become a modality of living for us—and not a forced one, simply the natural self-expression of ourselves as persons acted upon by truth.

Now the process repeats itself at another level. We can *try* to contemplate God as the loving persons we now are, but the results are scarce and poor. Once again, truth will have to alter us. How?

Experiencing the truth of the neighbor (loving him) is not a one-time breakthrough, just as humility is not. Constantly exposed to the neighbor as we are, we are constantly acted upon by the Spirit-inspired sympathy we manifest to him. It is crucial to realize that we continue to be "affected" by every movement of love that passes from us to the neighbor. We could say that *we* are more affected by it than the neighbor who receives it—he who loves is more transformed by the activity of loving than the one who is loved. What happens through this constant, long-term, sympathetic orientation to the other, says Saint Bernard, is that our experience of existence becomes egoless. As I said in the last conference, we become *similiter affecti*. (*Illorum vel bona vel mala tamquam propria sentiant*) (#6). The self is no longer the automatic point of reference in relating to reality, because the self is no longer a separate, discrete entity but a "sympathizer" (Hans Urs von Balthasar's definition of person).

This liberation purifies the heart once more, enough so that the person can be called "pure of heart." As pure of heart, he is now capable of being *affected* a third time, by Truth itself.

He could not "see" God before because he could not be touched by him, and he could not be touched by him, because his experience of reality remained self-referential. Now he is available to God whenever he wishes to give himself to him.

Contemplation, from our point of view, is not an activity. It is a *readiness*, an *openness* (not essentially different in "periods of prayer" than at any other moment) that has been brought about by having been transformed by the presence of truth mediated by human persons. In a way it could be affirmed that the person who is pure of heart is always contemplating. This is true in the sense that his heart is perpetually oriented in desire to the reception of Truth (*inquirimus contemplando*). At the same time, one of the most important assertions of Saint Bernard in this treatise is that particular graced experiences of the encounter with God as Truth are completely characterized by gratuitous initiative on God's part and brief and total transcendence of the ordinary conditions of being and knowing.

Saint Bernard's model here is Saint Paul. Paul had attained the first two heavens (humility and charity) "walking and being led" and in that sense there is a certain continuity between his spiritual history up to this point and what is to come. Now however, he is *raptus*—caught up to the third heaven of contemplation, to a place impossible for him to reach by any action or collaboration. What he undergoes there completely surpasses sensible experience, conceptual comprehension and verbal communication. It is eternal life that he is living, by God's gracious decision. Instead of "condescending" to Paul by the mediation of the Son and the Spirit, sent to act with and within men *within this world*, the Father, the divine mystery in its origin, lifts Paul up to himself (*ad tertium cælum per contemplationem exaltat; ad arcana veritatis rapiuntur*) (#23). That is why nothing can really be said, except in riddles and enigmas, about such experiences. Besides their being incommunicable by nature, they *impose an incommunicability*. They are given by God in predilection to a particular person, and they create in the recipient a supreme modesty: *Secretum meum mihi* ("My secret is mine," Is 24:16, Vulg., a favorite quotation of Bernard's).

The "possibility" of contemplation is given through the transformation effected by the truth of love; the truth of love becomes visible through the coming to grips with the truth of humility. For that reason, the would-be mystic should look to chapter seven of the Rule.

Conference 6

Divine Humility

Humility and pride as Saint Bernard sees them are so great that they cannot be lived out or displayed in their fullness by human beings. They don't have their origin in human beings and are not manifested in their full dimensions by human beings. Humility is most proper to God. God is humble, and the origin of humility, and the person who most personifies pride would be the devil. So in the first part of his treatise Saint Bernard shows us Christ as an icon of humility, and in the second part Lucifer as the icon of pride.

God saves humanity through his mercy. Saint Bernard has given us a universal principle: people become merciful through the experience of their own misery. Remember we saw it with the first truth, the truth which is yourself. The truth of yourself is your misery, and that misery enables you to say that all people have hang ups, including myself, and when you include yourself a door opens and your *affectus*, your sympathy, universalizes and you feel compassion not just for yourself but for all people. So the way to compassion is through misery, or in terms of the Beatitudes, the way to *misericordia* is through poverty of spirit. But, Saint Bernard asks, can we say that's true about God as well? Can we say he becomes merciful through the experience of his own misery? Is that a possible assertion or is it the one exception to the rule? Is God merciful without having been miserable, without having been made humble, or does he go through the same thing as we do and so becomes a model of the whole process instead of an exception to it? The answer that Bernard gives us is, yes,

God does become merciful in a new way so that his mercy may be effective. At some point in the treatise Saint Bernard says that to be merciful one has to go beyond *sentire* to *subvenire*. The Cistercians adored and kept all the flourishes of the Latin language, and one of their favorites was something that is called "assonance": two words that sound fundamentally similar but are used to describe realities that are similar but not identical. When they use "assonance" it is not a case of equals, but of two words that have something to do with each other. Or that are a little bit of a contrast, as in this case. So when Saint Bernard says that for mercy to be mercy it can't just be *sentire*, it has to be *subvenire*, this is what he means. *Sentire* is to feel sentiment; *subvenire*, to come to the aid of. He says it's not mercy when you see a movie about tragedy, a young child dying of cancer or something like that and use up three handkerchiefs and then you go to Friendly's. That's not mercy. That's a crying jag and an ice cream, it is not mercy. For it to be mercy, you have to do something. At the end of the film there is going to be a notice, "If you would like to really make this experience part of your life please mail a check to the American Cancer Society." If you get out your check book then that is mercy, because you have done something to help, you have not just had an emotive letting go. Saint Bernard says mercy is always like *that*, because *sentire* is a self-bounded experience. You don't touch the other person by crying, you haven't gone out of yourself, you are having an intrasubjective experience—it is you and your own affectivity. Sadness is the most attractive of the vices, I think, because it's like a warm blanket; feeling bad for yourself is delightful. So that's not mercy! Likewise, mercy doesn't just mean going out to help, because that still isn't mercy. It's only mercy when the person that you have gone out to help is really helped. Many of us have tried to help other people and the person hasn't accepted it or we haven't been able to present it well or some other obstacle has gotten in the way. For Saint Bernard it becomes truly mercy when the person has been transformed by your going out of yourself—it is ineffective short of that.

Somewhere in his writings, Saint Bernard has a little parable about mercy as a mother feeding her children, and he says that the mercy only happens when the child actually eats. The mother can prepare and cook the food, put the food on the plate, put the spoon up to the baby's mouth, but if the baby turns away his face, as babies frequently do when they are not in the mood, that's not mercy, because the nourishment has not gotten into the life of the child. The intention is merciful but the work of mercy, which is the alleviation of the child's hunger, has not yet occurred; only when the child swallows the food and grows is it mercy. So, God is merciful, and he has to find a way to turn his mercifulness into mercy. In other words, he has to find a way to make his mercy effective, and for it to be effective, it has to be received. From all eternity God is infinitely merciful, but his mercy is not *received* because his mercy is unable to be *perceived*. In his *Sermons on the Song of Songs*, Bernard sees this as exactly the motive for the Incarnation: God in his divine nature is inaccessible to us and cannot get his message across. And worst of all, he cannot get across to us what is the core of his heart—and what *is* the core of God's heart for Saint Bernard? *Benevolentia* and *humanitas. Benevolentia*: a lovingly disposed will. And *humanitas*—it is a wonderful pun because in classical Latin *humanitas* means two things: it means being a human person and it means being humane. So God as Spirit, because of our sin, is not able to tell us who he really is and how he really feels about us. He cannot communicate the thoughts of his heart—that's a phrase very, very frequently repeated in Saint Bernard, *cogitationes cordis eius*—he cannot get across the thoughts of his heart, which are thoughts of peace. He tries desperately, through the law and the prophets, to get these profound attitudes across to us but we are unable to see him or hear him because we are not pure of heart ("Blessed are the pure of heart because they shall perceive God"), and we, not being pure of heart, don't hear God saying, "I love you." We don't feel it; we don't sense that is God's attitude toward us. Even if we say that's how we feel, it isn't. And we go about forming all kinds of notions about him, Saint Bernard says in Sermon 6 on the Song of Songs. That God is hostile, God is indifferent, God is negligent. The one idea we are incapable of forming is that the transcendent God is really moved by our tragedy and wants to do everything in his infinite power to save us: that's what doesn't get through our skull before the Incarnation. We can say that each of us has to pass from the Old to the New Testament in his own existence as well, because it isn't so easy, even after Christ, to get it into our heads that God's fundamental dispositions toward us are love and mercy. Saint Bernard asks a rhetorical question in paragraph 12 of this treatise: When will we finally be able to see that unknown compassion which coexists with his impassability, which is eternal? When will we see that is how God is from everlasting to everlasting? In our experience, the context of which we are unable to transcend, compassion only rises from grievous suffering; only a person who has gone through hell can feel what we feel. What do we say so often when we try to console someone, and we try to do so as simply and delicately and nonpompously as possible? We go up to them and say, "I know." "I know" means, "I have been through it, I have been through something similar, I too am a man of sorrows. It is terrible what you are going through. You are not alone in it. You will come out of it because I have been through it and I have come out of it." All of that is communicated in the "I know." And we don't want to listen to someone who does not know. It is like those friends of Job. We simply cannot imagine that someone who has not been through the mill is going to be able to really feel for us. I think it is in his book on the Paschal Mystery that von Balthasar says, "Since the fall love is different than it was before the fall. Love has an element of pathos; love is indissolubly united with suffering." We measure love by suffering. We believe that someone loves us when they say, "I would die for you." That's how we know the person loves us, the willingness to undergo suffering, and the actual going through suffering we interpret as love. Love can be measured by the degree of suffering that someone is willing to undergo for our sake; von Balthasar says that's a consequence of the fall. Before that we could understand the love that came through blessedness, but this is a new ingredient. When I was a kid my father used to say to me every once in a while, "You know if this house was on fire, your mother would run back to get you." I said, "What about you, Daddy?" He said, "No." He said, "I would want to but I don't think that I would. I don't think I have it in me, but your mother would—I swear to you that she would. So if you are going to play with matches, do it while she is around."

Even if we could imagine a compassion that doesn't spring from a personal experience of suffering we would distrust it. My father who is now eighty-eight is starting to tell the same stories with a greater frequency. He always told the same stories even when his memory was completely functional, but now that it is diminishing he tells them with even more frequency. I remember as a kid his telling me a story. I don't agree with his outlook but I remember the story. He said, "Don't make friends with people in another class or rank than yourself." He said when he was in the army he was a sergeant, and there was a lieutenant who really liked him and wanted to become friends with him, and at some point he said, "No, there can't be any friendship between us; you are an officer and I'm not." I don't think it's right but I use this example. Like the buck private who instinctively does not patronize with officers, we miserable human beings cannot trust in a compassion that does not arise from suffering, from suffering and solidarity. There would be something terrible and dangerous about such compassion if it lacked the necessary basis of *communion in misfortune*. It's so easy for us to ask for help from Jesus crucified. You look at Jesus bleeding on the cross and it comes naturally to the lips and the heart to say, "Lord, have mercy." When we see God the Father sitting on his throne it doesn't come so easy to say, "God have mercy on me." Anything could come, but maybe not mercy, maybe not help, maybe not compassion. Psychologically it is very hard to ask for help, and we could not ask for help from such a source. But what does it matter if we understand God's mercy or not so long as he is merciful? Why doesn't God just save us whether we like it or not? For Bernard it is absolutely clear that there is no mercy until we open ourselves to receive it. Salvation occurs in the reception. Salvation occurs when we open ourselves up to God's mercy so that once again in communion with him we can be drawn out of our misery by his communication to us of his life and grace. I just reread a wonderful book on the Jesus prayer called *On the Power of the*

Name by Kallistos Ware. It really is wonderful, it is only twenty six pages, but worth reading and rereading. He says, "He who says to God, 'Have mercy,' laments his own helplessness, but voices at the same time a cry of hope. He speaks not only of sin but of its overcoming. He affirms that God accepts us though we are sinners, and that God asks from us in return to accept the fact that we are accepted." To accept the fact that we are accepted. That's when mercy becomes effective, not when God accepts us. That's the beginning. That's still not salvation. Salvation and mercy occur when we accept that we are accepted, and that's the harder part. I will tell you a story that illustrates this. When I was sixteen I was in a summer course in social sciences at Columbia run for high school juniors, and there was a very deep, profound and ultraserious Jewish guy from Chicago who was in the course. We used to take walks and one evening we took a walk—both of us were sixteen—and he said, "Let's tell each other the worst thing that we have ever done in our lives." I said, "Why would we want to do that?" He said, "Because we all live covered by seven veils, nobody knows anybody else, and so there cannot be genuine human friendship because there is all of this show and gauze and veil, and because of that there is no intimacy between persons. We should get beyond that." (There are still people in this world like people out of Dostoyevsky and he was one of them.) I said, "I don't think I want to do that." He said, "No. We are going to do it." "Okay, you go first." So he told me the worst thing he had done. To me it didn't seem very much of anything. He then said, "Do you still accept me?" I said, "Yes, I accept you." "You can be my friend?" I said, "I am your friend." "This doesn't change anything." "No." "Okay, your turn." So I told him, and when I concluded my story about the worst thing I've ever done, he said, "I can't be your friend anymore." I said, "Excuse me!" He said, "Not if you did that. I couldn't be a friend of a person who has done something like that, but I appreciate your transparency and I do wish you all the best." That's the last time we ever spoke. And not only did we have to get through the summer course together; we went to the same university and we spent four years together and we never spoke again. To me it's worthwhile recounting, because that's our fear. It's so hard to accept that we are accepted, because we are waiting for a lightning bolt to come, and to believe that we are accepted by God, that's harder for some reason. So how is God going to get beyond this blockage? His mercy, which cannot rest until it has freed us from our wretchedness, freely takes on our wretchedness. For Saint Bernard that's why God becomes man. To become miserable. To become miserable and to learn again experientially what he always knew in his divinity. To learn feelingly what he always knew divinely. To feel compassion for us that arises out of experience, human experience, and not just out of divine tenderness—because that's how we can process it. How many times in the Bernardine corpus does he give a resume of the sufferings of the incarnate Son of God: preaching by day, praying by night, suffering hunger, cold and fatigue, insulted and spat upon, hanging on the cross, pale with the pallor of death. In fact, through the assumption of our nature, God in Christ *does* come to experience human misery firsthand, and the experience of this misery gives rise to a form of mercy that cannot be had by any other way: by that mode of knowing which can only be learned by the limitations of the flesh *(illo dumtaxat modo cognitionis, quem docet defectio carnis)* (#12). It's a new ballgame for God in Christ to come to mercy through that misery, which opens us up to the sufferings of others. Now he can say, "I know." And now we can say, "I know that you know because I can see you as the Man of Sorrows."

With this, God's mercy gains credibility. Just as in the second sermon *On the Song of Songs*, humanity cries out at the Incarnation, "This at last is a God bone of my bone and flesh of my flesh," here the sight of Christ suffering his passion in compassion for us leads us to confidence and self-entrustment: we see his suffering, and we see that the sufferings are an expression of his mercy, and so we open up. Saint Bernard says, "Let not the frail children of Adam hesitate any longer to entrust their infirmities to him. Because now not only *can* he heal them as God, not only does he *want* to heal them as our neighbor, but now he *knows them because he has gone through them*" (#9). In the case of us human beings, *we* have to go through the experience of wretchedness so that *we* may come to feel any degree of compassion for the neighbor. In the case of Christ on the other hand *he* has to go through misery, not so that he may feel compassion, but so that we may feel confidence (*non illi, ut dixi, scientia, sed nobis fiducia crevit*) (#9). It really is a replay of that second sermon *On the Song of Songs*. Maybe it is good to give a reminder. In the second sermon of the *Song of Songs*, humanity is crying out for a redeemer, sinful humanity is crying out for a redeemer and the prophets are saying a redeemer is coming, a redeemer is coming, and humanity is becoming impatient and says, "Shut up. We have already heard you say this for centuries and no redeemer has come." Then finally comes the Incarnation and humanity is not satisfied, because the Incarnate One is the Son of God and humanity says, "Send us another one." And God Incarnate says, "What's the matter with me?" And humanity says, "The problem with you is that you are God." "Well yes, I am the Son of God. What's the matter with that? That gives me all the power necessary to redeem you." "Yes, but it means that you are on *His* side." Salvation here is seen as a process of reconciliation between God and mankind. So it's like having two prosecutors. It is like the defense lawyer is in the secret pay of the prosecutor, of the district attorney. We don't want that—send us somebody else. And Christ has to convince humanity that he is just as human as he is divine, and finally humanity lets itself be convinced and cries out, "Okay. It is true; you are flesh of flesh and bone of bone. You can go through our suffering so you can be our advocate." It is the same thing here: mercy can only be accepted from one who is human.

It is all a matter of *proximity*. Saint Bernard does not say there is a greater sum total of mercy in God after the Incarnation than before. But what has changed is that there is now in us a sense of safety and intimacy that enables us to be vulnerable to God in Christ: *non dico ut sapientior efficeretur, sed propinquior videretur* (#9). A Dominican Old Testament scholar, who taught at Fribourg, said that the worst consequence of original sin is that our basic response to God is fear. The closer God comes the less we like it. That's the whole significance of Adam hiding when God goes for the afternoon stroll. Instead of going out to greet him as before, he runs for the bushes. This professor says, and I'm sure that he's right, we have a tendency to think that death is the worst consequence, or the expulsion from Eden, or many other things, the fact that we have to work to earn our living by the sweat of our brow, but that's not it. He says the worst consequence is that God provokes fear. Saint Bernard says this also when he says that in the beginning of the spiritual life our relationship to God is that of servant to master. Bernard says something very striking: God always wears the mask that corresponds to the face that we put on him and the face that we put on ourselves. If we experience God as a master, we will be a slave; if we experience God as a paymaster, we will be a hireling. If we experience God as a father, we will be a son, as a teacher we will be a disciple, as a bridegroom we will be a bride. But in the beginning of the spiritual life, before we have learned about his mercy in Christ, God is the big boss. I have a great love for squirrels. But squirrels are to us as we are to God except for very rare cases of tame ones in Central Park. At least the ones in Novo Mundo are—and I think all over the world. If you go out of your way to find some delicious nuts for them to eat and crack them open and hold out your hand and say, "Here squirrel, squirrel, squirrel," they are not going to run in your direction. The fear of you is stronger than the love of the nuts, so off they run. And that is our relationship with God also until the Incarnation.

In response to a question about how Jewish people experience the mercy of God without faith in the mystery of the Incarnation:

What a Jewish person is called to, in his particular process of spiritual growth and maturation, is to come to see that God the Father is the merciful one. There are two central attributes of God the Father in Jewish biblical spirituality—truth and compassion, truth and love, *hesed v'rahamim*. It is true that we finally got the message through the passion and resurrection of Jesus. But Jesus was giving the message all through his ministry and he was not talking about himself but talking about the Father. All of those

parables are parables about the merciful Father. Beginning with
the prodigal son and with the workmen in the vineyard who will
all be paid the same thing, and the man who pardons the immense debt of the servant who says, "Just give me time." And
instead of just giving him time he gives him a complete remission
of the debt. There's also that wonderful tongue-in-cheek parable
in Luke about the unjust judge who is God the Father where the
underlying message is that God is waiting to show mercy on us.
That certainly is Hassidic spirituality, the God of infinite tenderness and compassion, and the God who suffers with us. Remember yesterday when I finished my talk, Father Francis Michael*
said, "Thank you for the midrash." I do not know if everybody
knows what midrash is. It is one of the basic components of the
Talmud, the Talmud is that oral law which took centuries to put
together and was finally written down three centuries after
Christ. One of the basic components is commentaries on the Law,
and another basic component are anecdotes—rethinking and
retelling the stories of the Old Testament. One of the most famous
has to do with the Passover. The Jews have crossed the Red Sea
dry shod and finally after 400 years of slavery they are on their
way to the Promised Land. They are out of the grip of Pharaoh;
he can never touch them again. And so the angels have a party
and they are singing and dancing and blowing their trumpets
and some are playing their harps and at a certain point in the
party they recognize that the guest of honor is not there. God!
Where is he? So they go looking for him. Didn't he know there
was a party, we told him and it is basically in his honor, and finally after a long search they find him and where is he? He is in
a corner crying. The angels are annoyed beyond belief. "What is
the matter with you? We have spent four hundred years figuring
how to get these people out of Egypt. It took everything. It took
plagues, it took Moses, it took this, it took that, it took opening
the Red Sea, huffing and puffing and blowing the sea across into
pieces and finally it worked and you're crying! How can you be

* Don Francis Michael Stiteler, current abbot of Holy Spirit Abbey, Conyers.
Ed.

crying when the chosen people are saved and not a single one of them was lost?" And he says, "I'm crying for my children the Egyptians that were drowned in the Red Sea." Now that's a wonderful intuition of the mercy of God, the universal mercy of God, but it's hard to get there and stay there, both for the Jew and for the Christian.

Here is another anecdote that shows how hard it is. My sister was initially tremendously against my entering the monastery. I had come to see her and my brother-in-law before going into Spencer and I ask to speak to my brother-in-law first because he's going to help me get my sister to accept it. So we have a talk and she is knocking at the door, "Can I come in now?" "Okay come in." She looks at my brother-in-law's face and says to me, "You have cancer." "I don't have cancer." "My husband doesn't have a face like that for nothing. You have six months to live." I said, "I don't have cancer and God willing I have more than six months to live." "Well, what is it? What's going on?" I said, "I'm going into the monastery." "That's worse than cancer." So the day came for me to go into the monastery and she said, "We are driving you there." I said, "Please don't. I don't want you to." She said, "Why?" I said, "Because it is going to be an awful experience for you and it is also going to be an awful experience for me. I want to go to the monastery happy. So why don't we just kiss at your house and friends of mine will drive me up." "No, we are taking you." "Okay." So we got into the car, it was a Sunday, and she said, "I assume you went to mass." I said, "Yes, I did." She said, "Let me hear what the gospel was." So I told her the gospel and the gospel was about the workers in the vineyard. She's a smart cookie. She has never read the New Testament but she's really bright. Halfway through the story she said, "Don't tell me anymore. I know how it ends." I said, "You couldn't know how it ends." She said, "I know how it ends." I said, "Okay, tell me." She said, "They all finish, they come back and you know what? They all get the same pay." I said, "You've never read that?" She said, "No I've never read that. But is that how it ends?" I said, "That's how it ends." She said, "That's why I could never become a Christian. It's a religion for crazy people." Deep down

Jews and Christians meet. It can be just as hard for us Christians to believe that Christ—especially the glorified Christ—is truly compassion, as it is for the Jews to believe that God is merciful.

In Brazil, sometimes I've found that I've had to accept becoming temporarily heterodox in order to get this point across. Occasionally I run into somebody there who says, "The only God I can believe in is Our Lady." That's a very Brazilian statement, with its maternal feeling. I know what they mean: God is terrifying and condemning, whether it is the Father, the Son or the Holy Spirit. Not one of the three can be trusted, and the only person they can have confidence in is Our Lady. So they say, "So now what? Do I have to leave the monastery?" I say, "No, pray to Our Lady." "But Our Lady isn't God." I say, "For the time being she is for you. She will take you to her Son and the Son will take you to the Father and you will get to everywhere you have to get to, but for now Our Lady is it." It is very interesting for those who know Ignatian spirituality: at the end of every meditation on the Gospel you begin by praying to Our Lady to take you to her Son. Then you go on praying to the Son and asking him to take you to the Father. Ignatius was a Latin. It makes sense.

In his treatise *On Loving God*, Saint Bernard talks about a tremendous battle between fear and love which we know is a continuum which is so important to him and our fear as to what will happen if we give ourselves to God. Terrifying! And so we take an absolutely firm position with the two feet of our will, and we say, "I will be generous with God, I will give a lot to God, I'll give everything to God, but not myself to God." And Saint Bernard says that nothing can get us beyond that, except the contemplation of Christ crucified. If we really look at God's love for us in Christ, the supreme icon of which is the cross, he says, we can't maintain that position anymore, we find ourselves pulled out of ourselves and beyond ourselves into that gift of ourselves. And it's wonderful! In the treatise—I think in numbers seven and eight—immediately following that, Saint Bernard places us in the garden of the resurrection. It is almost like a dream sequence that takes place. Contemplating the crucifixion, there comes a tremendously painful moment when the will to keep ourselves for ourselves is overcome. We are ripped out of ourselves and given over to Christ. And then all of a sudden we are in a garden with flowering trees and fruit trees, and it is both the garden of paradise and the garden of the resurrection. And of course that is what happens if you let your heart be pulled out of your body. It happens because looking at Jesus on the cross you see love in its infinite form. I like to say it, and I think it is true, that Saint Bernard's soteriology is one of *showing*. Fundamentally, for Bernard, Christ does not save us by pain, by ransoming, by redeeming. He saves us by manifesting God's love in a way that cannot be said, that cannot be expressed in words. His whole life says it is that way, and it is the showing that converts us and saves us. Because for Bernard perdition consists in not believing in the love God has for us, and salvation in believing in the love God has for us. And it is the Incarnation and especially its culmination in the Paschal Mystery that undeniably shows that love for us.

Back to the main point: It's not a question of a greater sum total of mercy than before but a sense of intimacy which enables us to be vulnerable to God in Christ. "I do not say that he became wiser but that he has come to seem closer."

In the conclusion of his *excursus* on the humble Christ, Bernard shows the continuity and interrelationship of the two modes of his mercy, the eternal mercy and the temporal/experiential mercy: "If that mercy which does not know misery had not existed first, if God were not eternally merciful, the Incarnation would never have taken place and he never would have had the experience of the second kind of mercy which has misery as its mother. If he had not come to the second kind, he would not have been able to attract us to himself. Had he not been able to draw us to himself, he could not have drawn us out from the lake of misery and the miry deep." (*Si illa, quae miseriam nescit, misericordia non praecessisset, ad hanc, cuius miseria mater est, non accessisset. Si non accessisset, non attraxisset; si non attraxisset, non extraxisset. Unde enim extraxit, nisi de lacu miseriæ et de luto fæcis?*) (#12) There has been a wonderful multiplication of mercy, Saint Bernard says: to the age-old has been added the new and never before known. This treatise is famous because it got Bernard in hot water. It got him in hot water exactly because of this idea that Christ could learn something by experience, the idea that God was capable of transformative experience. And so this treatise begins with a *retractatio* which is a kind of little apology and defence at the same time. He's not going to take back what he says because it is the core of the treatise, divine mercy in the incarnate Christ is the core of the treatise, but he is going to explain that if you want to look at it mathematically it is not that God's wisdom is greater than it was before or his mercy greater, but that a new modality has been added. He did learn, in his humanity, from what he experienced. Yet, without the sum of his *scientia* becoming greater. I think today we can feel free to wonder whether Bernard was not somehow stretching toward something even further, the idea of Christ learning, not simply in another mode but from scratch, in his humanity. Unquestionably that earlier divine, eternal mercy was the motive for the Incarnation and continued to be the guiding force of his life. We can rightly say that Jesus is the incarnation of the eternal mercy of God. But perhaps we can say that the humility of the Incarnation, even more than being the experience of *miseria*, of misery, was the beautiful experience of progressively understanding and relating to the world. Being changed and deepened by one's encounter with it.

Thus, in this way, coming up against the misery of others really would have evinced compassion in Jesus, more and more as he grew to see what it did to people and how in the plan of God there was a way out of it. I think that we can, even without going outside the lines of orthodoxy, include the idea of a misery in Jesus that stemmed from his human experiences of disappointment and frustration and that also generated mercy toward others.

(There is a beautiful little book on Mark by the French philosopher and Scripture scholar Ghislain Lafont, that some of you must know. He speaks about a Galilean springtime, a time in Jesus' ministry when it seemed to him that everyone was accepting his mission, and the joy that that generated in him, that the kingdom of God was being received: "Go and tell John the blind are seeing, the lame are walking, the poor hearing the good news and blessed are those who are not scandalized in me." And Lafont says at a certain point Jesus perceived that the tide had changed and that rather than there being a fundamental acceptance, there was a growing opposition, and he says what a source of frustration and misery that must have been to Jesus, because everything that he had come to give was being thrown back at him rather than being received. So I think it is not hard for us today to see exactly what Saint Bernard is using is a universal principle, that the sorrow of Jesus' own heart, the frustration of his own plan, which was not self-centered, but was his plan, which was the desire of his heart—to communicate the kingdom to others—that this too became a source of compassion.)

At any rate, the humility of Christ as described by Saint Bernard remains a model for us. It is a humility oriented from the beginning to mercy. Whatever experience of *miseria* he may have had, it always immediately transcended itself into sensitivity to the misery of others and a willingness to pay any personal price to save them from it. In this beautiful book of Kierkegaard that I cited, *Works of Love*, he has a wonderful commentary on Jesus looking at Peter after Peter's betrayal. Kierkegaard says, "What was the content of that glance? Was it the hurt feelings of having been betrayed by the person who had just sworn he would always be with him? Was it, 'I told you so' because he had told him so? Was it, *Et tu, Brute?*, that is, 'Nobody can be trusted, not even you?' Was it the unbearable pain of having had up to now at least one person who was with him in his trials and now there was nobody?" And Kierkegaard says, "No. It isn't about Jesus' suffering from the betrayal of Peter. Jesus saw Peter's betrayal of him as a tremendous danger signal—danger for Peter. That betrayal could be the end of him. Peter could be irreparably broken by what he had done, because in betraying the love he had for this man Jesus, his master, he had also radically betrayed himself. Peter could go out and do the same thing that Judas did." And so Kierkegaard says that the look of Jesus to Peter was a look that said, "Listen, we will clear up the details later. I love you." Isn't that fabulous! He looked at Peter to console Peter, and Kierkegaard says that's why Peter wept, not because he had betrayed Christ but because his betrayal had elicited even more love. Many of you must know the famous saying of Saint Teresa of Avila, "God tortures me. How? Every time I sin he punishes me by shedding more graces on me. That's the only kind of punishment I have ever experienced from God." And this is the mercy of Jesus. His misery always immediately transcended itself into a sensitivity to the misery of others and the willingness to pay any personal price to save them from that misery. The glance at Peter is one case, and the incomparable example of it is his prayer on the cross for his executioners. He transformed his suffering into compassion for those who crucified him. Jesus, the incarnate mercy of God became the humility of God: Jesus, divine humility. I don't know if you know that in the Orthodox tradition that is one of the great icons. It's an icon of Holy Saturday. I'm not talking about the famous icon of Jesus descending into hell to save Adam and Eve and trampling on the gates of hell. That's the first of the Easter icons. The Holy Saturday icon is of Jesus both dead and alive in his sepulchre, standing with his arms stretched out and his eyes closed. And the name of that icon is Extreme Humility. If you can get to see a copy of it, it is really worth contemplating.

Conference 7

The Trinity Saves the Trinity

Once again for Saint Bernard life in Christ, especially in the monastic context, consists of three truths. The truth of ourselves, which is humility, the truth of relationship with the neighbor which is compassion and the truth of the knowledge of God which is contemplation. Three experiences of truth: our own truth, the neighbor's truth and God's truth. Also called humility, charity and contemplation. For Saint Bernard, this process of the monk's attaining to humility, charity and contemplation is not something alongside his being saved in Christ. It's not an *aspect* of salvation. It *is* his being saved in Christ. For Saint Bernard, to become humble, compassionate, and then united to God in contemplation, that is the process of our being saved in Christ through the monastic charism. Being saved in Christ, considered in its whole sweep from conversion to confirmation in grace.

Saint Bernard, along with the whole patristic tradition, sees our redemption as a work of the whole Trinity. So this process of attaining to humility, charity and contemplation will be a work of the whole Trinity. All three persons will be involved. They're always at work creating us, governing us, saving us, glorifying us. In this bringing us to humility, charity and contemplation the three divine persons evidently work in harmony, but likewise work distinctly. Saint Bernard expresses the collaboration and difference in the oxymoron (a contradiction in terms) *"divisa individuæ Trinitatis operatio"*—"the divided working of the undivided Trinity" (#20). So each of the persons of the Trinity will work in his own particular way to bring about that salvation which is the attainment of the three truths, but that working will be a working in collaboration, distinct but in harmony. In a beautiful intuition Saint Bernard asserts that the Persons of the Trinity save us by uniting themselves to us. That is how we are saved. We speak a lot about "union of spirit" but for Saint Bernard the union here is with each one of the persons of the Trinity. It is that that saves us and it is that which brings us to these three truths. The three persons of the Trinity form "*conjunctions*" with us. There is a new union between us and each of the persons of the Trinity.

While this is a marvellous condescension on God's part, it also has a certain naturalness, since in our interiority (where, for Bernard, we are most ourselves) we also have a trinitarian structure. Not only are we *capax Dei*, not only are we receptive to God as was explained in a previous conference; we are trinitarianly *capax Dei*.

This threefold receptivity, this Trinitarian receptivity consists of the three *faculties* of the soul: reason, will and memory. It's important to understand that reason, will and memory are a Trinitarian family themselves. You can't pull them apart from each other. It's also important to say that they are not an *aspect* of our interiority. They *are* our interiority. One of the heresies which Saint Bernard opposed was the idea that above the three Persons of the Trinity was God. There was the Father, the Son and the Holy Spirit and then there was the Godhead who contained the Trinity, coordinated the Trinity, kept the Trinity going and was superior to the Trinity. That, says Saint Bernard is not true and I as a Catholic agree with him. There's nothing else in the Trinity except Father, Son and Holy Spirit. There is no fourth principle that coordinates or harmonizes. The same thing is true of our rational soul, to use the language of the Cistercian Fathers. We are reason, will and memory; that is our interior identity. There is not a fourth center to which all these three belong and that coordinates them. We are this trinitarian interaction of reason, will and memory. Already Saint Augustine had made the link between the Trinity of divine Persons and the trinity of spiritual faculties, reason, will and memory, and this correlation was steadfastly maintained by the Cistercian Fathers in their treatises on the soul.

It turns out that the personal history of monastic salvation (which is humility, charity, contemplation) is the reproduction in our faculties of God's universal saving plan. Salvation for each of us, as Saint Bernard sees it, begins with the mission of the Son, his Incarnation. The Son as Word and Wisdom comes precisely to unite himself to us with our *reason*. The mission of the Son, the sending of the Son, the contribution of the Son to this salvific process in us is the union with our reason. It must be so, since it is our reason that is capable of being illumined and conformed to divine intelligence. Christ, Divine Word and Wisdom Incarnate, offers himself to our reason both by word and example (one thinks of the abbot's teaching) and delivers us from an "exteriorized" understanding of reality. To such an extent does he come to permeate and enlighten our reason that it becomes serviceable and trustworthy as his representative: Saint Bernard says that Christ comes to use our reason as his vicar (*utens tamquam pro se vicaria*) (#21). There is born a real and progressive unity, a marriage as he says in the commentary *On the Song of Songs*, between the divine wisdom and our human reason. Our human reason is no longer simply human reason, it is enlightened human reason, illumined human reason, and first of all it is corrected human reason, it is undistorted human reason. That illusion and that distortion through which we see reality because of our pride are removed. So this is the first major aspect of our being saved: the Word is sent to us, it unites itself to us, it informs our reason, our reason begins to glow with it and our reason begins to think with it. It's *our* reason; it is not a case of brainwashing. It is our reason but it is our reason united with the divine intellect, which is what it was made to be. Remember our reason is that receptivity, every one of the faculties is receptivity to God in a specific way and our reason is receptivity to God as truth.

The sign that this first salvific occurrence is taking place, says Saint Bernard, is when we begin to judge ourselves by means of our reason. When I was a first-year novice in Spencer, a course was given on the Golden Age of Liturgy, the fourth century, the great liturgical doctors of the Church, and especially in the Greek tradition. The course was being given by a priest who was a junior professed, he had been a priest before he entered, and I found myself questioning, giving counter examples, disagreeing, taking the reins of the class for myself at one point or another. He was very good, I was not very good and I remember feeling terrific about myself, but then at one point my reason illumined by Christ posed a simple question: "Why are you behaving this way?" And the answer that came was, "Because you are an arrogant SOB"—and that was the truth. I hope it is a little less of the truth now than it was twenty-five years ago. Saint Bernard says that one of the surest signs that this marriage between the Word and our reason is taking place is that we are able to look inward and to understand who we are, why we say and do and think and feel as we do. Reason has straightened out the kinks in the justification and the explanations we give for our behaviors and our reactions.

Saint Bernard says that the more this goes on, the more our reason becomes objective rather than defensive or subjectifying. What matters more and more is the truth, because reason being what it is has an insatiable love for the truth, and as Christ's divine reason unites itself with our human reason truth becomes the all-desirable object of this particular faculty. This happens to such an extent that in a conflict between our reason and the truth, our reason takes the truth's side rather than our side. Saint Bernard says that our reason starts to exercise the office of truth against itself. It's a lovely process which requires a certain peace. It takes a certain self-awareness and a certain fearlessness to let that union of the divine reason with our reason occur to such an extent that, in the famous words I quoted already of the Abba Zosima, we don't lie to ourselves about ourselves, and if a lie begins to come up we catch it almost immediately and say, "Now don't kid yourself. If you want to sin you go right ahead and sin but don't say that you're doing it for your grandmother's sake. You are doing it because that's what you want at the moment." When this union between the Word and the reason becomes stable and complete, what is born, says Saint Bernard, is humility, the resulting *coniunctio* is humility: *Ex qua prima coniunctione Verbi et rationis, humilitas nascitur* (#21). It is no longer an external judgment; it has been (in psychological terms) "interiorized." Reason ends up becoming so objective that it takes truth's side rather than *our* side (*contra se Veritatis fungatur officio*) (#21).

This mission of the Son, of the Word, of Divine Reason terminates with his death and resurrection: and this too has to do with truth because we know that one of the aspects of the crucifixion is that it is God's judgment on sin. When we accept the crucifixion we see on the cross sin judged, and what sin leads to, and our involvement in sin. So the cross is truth: it is the truth of what we bring ourselves to by the way we live when we live alienated from God. And so is the resurrection truth because the resurrection is God's justification of the sinner. "Christ died for our sins and was raised up for our justification:" cross and resurrection are truth. This is what happens microcosmically when in humility our conscience condemns us (we can therefore see that monastic humility is not something "light") and we learn to place our confidence in God rather than ourselves. This marriage between the Word and our reason intensifies up until the moment of our death. Many of you must know Benedict Groeschel, through reading him or through meeting him. He gave the retreat at Spencer many years ago and I was going through a period where I was feeling a lot of envy about a person in the community. It was really something eating away at me, and at times it led me into definite unkindness in speech and certainly in thought and feeling, so I said, "I'm going to take advantage of this and ask to speak with Father Benedict." We took a walk up North Hill and I told him the whole story with tears, and I remember that his first comment after I stopped talking was, "Yup, that's about the top of the middle." I said, "You mean there are worse things than that?" "Oh yes, you're just getting started, kid." That was about twenty years ago and he was right.

Here is a story about the defences the reason can erect against the attempts of the Truth to unite itself to it. I once gave spiritual direction to a person who was convinced that he was dying of AIDS. I knew this person pretty well and I knew there was no way the person could be dying of AIDS because it can only be contracted in a certain number of ways. That person had never been involved in any of these ways, but the person agonized for months that he was dying of AIDS. I went to see the psychologist that worked with the Spencer candidates, to speak to him about a particular candidate, and I decided to mention the situation. I told him the story and he said, "Okay, you're smart. What do you think is going on?" I said, "Well, as a matter of fact, I do have a theory." He said, "What's your theory?" I said, "The theory is that, deep down, this is a consolation for him." He asked me in what way. I responded, "Deep, deep down this person knows that he doesn't have AIDS, so to think that he does does not really create fear or anxiety. There is something scarier that he cannot face, and so in order not to face that he's invented a fear that has no objective grounding to it. It is much simpler to live with. He blots out the genuine fear by a fear of something that he knows can never happen."

The marriage between the Word and the reason is an ongoing process and that is why we cannot force self-knowledge but only take it as it comes. I have told you different stories about myself, such as laughing at the subcantor and all that, but evidently I have not told you everything about myself. And I would go so far as to say that there is still a huge amount about myself that I myself am unaware of, for good but also for bad. Self-knowledge can't be anticipated. Because God is kindness, he has coordinated it and we come to it only to the extent that we can tolerate it. This extreme humility, of which the Orthodox iconographic tradition speaks, evidently has to be something like being crucified. The icon is a pictorial representation of this. And so from this marriage of the Word and reason humility is born.

In response to a question about the difficulty of coming to experience the union between Christ the Word and our reason:

There is a beautiful passage in the writing of Saint Edith Stein where she says that it's very hard to be led into the way of the holiness of the gospel, but thanks be to God, once you're in, it is almost impossible to be drawn out of it. And what I would say is this: that in the beginning of the monastic life, in the first couple of years, usually we do go through some tremendous battle with the truth. The truth of ourselves, the truth of Christ, the truth of our commitment and that's the anguish of the novitiate. Many times God gives us the grace to persevere through it and if we do persevere through it, from that point onward we are never completely ignorant about the truth, whether we choose it or not. If we have gone through that first very difficult union with the truth, in the future, if we are going against the truth in a small thing or a great thing we feel malaise, we feel uncomfortable. It could be on the bodily level, it could be on the emotional level, it could be intellectual, but we feel that something wrong is about to happen, we are about to do something that is not fully true. I think *that's* why it's so hard to have that initial marriage with the truth as something painful—because it is new, because it's unknown—but once that first great experience has happened we have a certain radar. Even if we can't verbalize why something is not true we intuit it. Once that marriage has started, that truth is there permanently. It is like what Jesus said in Saint John's gospel about the presence of the Holy Spirit who guides us into all truth and also tells us when we are about to veer away from it.

In response to a question concerning the story about the person who thought he had AIDS:

This is a light that came to me in my novitiate. I often say to the novices and juniors, and I think it's in line with the desert tradition also, that *knowledge* or in this context *truth* is automatically curative. It is the tendency of the demons, our neurosis, our untruthfulness to hide itself—that passage we heard that whoever sins hides from the light because he doesn't want his deeds to be known and he doesn't want himself to be known, including by himself. Let's say that that pseudofear was unmasked as being groundless and the person was being guided toward an encounter with the real source of fear. The anxiety level should go way up, but he's onto something and onto something real and that means that it is not the sickness unto death, because he's coming closer to the truth and the fear is a sign that the approximation

is taking place. It's things like that that make vocation discern-
ment so difficult, because it can look like a person is coming apart.
Here is something deeper about myself. My first year in the novitiate was very difficult and my novice master had decided that
I should go home. Not because I was doing anything scandalous
but simply because it was too hard for me. He consulted his
spiritual director, who was a psychiatrist, Father Raphael, and
Father Raphael said, "Let him be, he's going to get through it."
So that's another important point. During the whole context of
spiritual direction the spiritual director also has to learn not to
be afraid, because sometimes things will happen in people, especially in moments of great conversion or encounter with the
truth or with the life of Christ in us that will require a certain
destructuring of the person. You need a lot of wisdom and practice to see what is happening—a breakthrough or a breakdown.
And if you make a mistake, it could get serious.

We come now to the mission of the Spirit. The mission of the
Spirit consists in his being poured as love into the hearts of those
who have come to humbly believe. Into the heart, Saint Bernard
would say, means into the will. Because just as the Logos, Divine
Truth, unites himself with our reason so the Holy Spirit, who is
love, Divine Love, unites himself with our will. The will is the
faculty receptive and responsive to divine charity and so this is
the second union. The second union is the union of the Spirit
with our will. Prior to the coming of the Spirit, the will broods
over itself, limits itself to itself. Instead of saying "I love because
I love," as in that famous saying of Saint Bernard, it says, "I love
myself because I love myself." The will is bent back onto itself.
Infected by a poison of the flesh (*veneno quidem carnis infectam*)
(#21), the will declares its love for itself in a parody of Saint Bernard's cry. But now, as I have already mentioned in other conferences, the Spirit uniting himself to our will universalizes the
will's natural tenderness. Baldwin of Ford in that wonderful
treatise on the cenobitic life says that the sign of the gift of the
Holy Spirit is its unstoppable dynamism: any gift given by the
Holy Spirit to enrich us spiritually passes through us to others

and to others and others and others. The Spirit is God's self-communication as love, and so when we receive any genuine gift of the Spirit we should feel an irresistible urge to communicate that gift further. If that desire, if that spontaneity, is not there, if we do not find ourselves loving our neighbor as ourself, then we can be sure it's not the Spirit who is at work. So the Spirit universalizes the will's natural tenderness. Now it is "natural" for the will to be tender to all, says Saint Bernard, including the person's enemies. And as we know, in the monastic tradition, love of one's enemies is always the ultimate test of charity. There is an anecdote I was told in my novitiate: one Russian elder asked another Russian elder, "How can I know when I have reached contemplative prayer?" And the answer given was, "You know you have reached contemplative prayer when, after having prayed, the next time you think of your enemy it is with peace and love." If the thought of your enemy brings disturbance or resentment or desire for revenge you have not yet reached pure prayer. You have not reached contemplation. And pure prayer means prayer in the Spirit. It means prayer *of* the Spirit, it means the Spirit praying in us. So as I have already cited in a well-known and lovely image, Saint Bernard compares the effect of the Spirit in our wills to that of oil on a skin: just as a skin anointed with oil expands, so the person who has been covered with the celestial unction finds that his affectionateness extends even to love of enemies: *ita ut more pellis, quæ uncta extenditur, ipsa quoque unctione perfusa cælesti, usque ad inimicos per affectum dilatetur* (#21). Clearly, the perfection of this second union, as the Holy Spirit enters into the will and conforms it to himself, is divine charity.

Our third faculty is our *memory*. Memory is a very difficult word to translate because it has one fixed meaning in the Middle Ages, and another very fixed and different meaning in the age in which we live now. In the twelfth century it means a habitual consciousness, it means our underlying consciousness, it also means the whole archive of our experience. Our self-possession, our focus, our mode of consciousness, our awareness—and all of this the Father unites to himself by contemplation. So the first marriage is between the Word, divine reason and our reason, the second marriage is between the Holy Spirit and our will and that marriage is love. And the third is between the Father and our memory, and that is contemplation. Liturgically speaking we can say our salvation is not complete either at Easter when the Word completes his mission, nor at Pentecost, when the Spirit completes his mission, but in our final glorification. This glorification is anticipated and begun in certain moments of rapture, which we call mystical experience. In these moments the reason's focus on itself and the will's affection for the neighbor are temporarily suspended: they don't function. "At these moments" says Saint Bernard, "the reason is not permitted to think of itself, focus on itself, and the will is incapable of focusing on the neighbor" (*ita ut nec ratio de se, nec voluntas de proximo cogitare sinatur*) (#21). What happens is that the Father "glues" the memory to himself. The word he uses is *conglutinare*. Bernard makes a paste and he binds the memory so intensely to himself that God is the only possible focus of our attention, of our absolute and our undivided attention as we say.

The Father so glues the memory to himself as his spouse that the memory is nothing but a rapturous being in the presence of. That is, the whole person is simply enraptured in being in the presence of, with no other awareness; in an awareness that's filled with love, but love is not felt as a separate experience: it is one single experience. Understanding is not a felt experience either; the rapture goes completely beyond the ordinary functioning of the intelligence or the reason. That's why he said they are suspended; the only thing that functions is the memory, this essential awareness, which is completely fixed on God.

Saint Bernard uses here a verse of the Canticle to describe this experience: "The King has led me into his bedchamber" (Song 1:4). Even when such experiences are not taking place—which is the majority of the time (the experiences themselves are exceptional and brief: *modicum; hora videlicet quasi dimidia*—evidently this does not refer to "clock time"), the union between the Father and the memory perdures, and the memory in its more everyday functioning finds its delight and nourishment in musing over what it has been given: *postmodum memoria ad se reditura pascatur* (#21). When the memory returns to itself and feeds on its experience, to some small extent it can even find joy in sharing these experiences with others who have passed through them. Yet because of the nuptial nature of these experiences, they impose a certain modesty, and the soul's most natural response when asked about them is, "My secret is my own" (*Secretum meum mihi,* #22). William of Saint Thierry, speaking autobiographically about the same phenomenon, says that there is a persistence in the memory of these experiences, but when he tries to describe exactly what it is that persists in the memory, the content can't be unpacked. It's such a dense and single experience because it's an experience of the transcendent God, and you can't give details about it—it has no details. You can't give aspects to it, because it has no aspects. You can return to it in joy and maybe even say something very vague about it or something inspired by it. William says that "it remains in the memory as embers of thought and these thoughts keep holiday in the soul." I think that is a very beautiful phrase, this idea of an inner feast with what is left behind after such an experience. Something within us still keeps festival because of that kind of unitive experience of God and the memory, which is contemplation, which is the third truth.

Remember, all of this for Saint Bernard is the outcome of humility. None of this would happen, neither charity nor contemplation, unless we let the Word tell us about ourselves and unite itself with the reason. This is the best sales pitch of all, this is what makes humility worth it: the idea that such a thing can and does happen.

It's important to say that this is not an artificial schema on the part of Saint Bernard. I believe that we do live successively with the three persons of the Trinity in the order that Saint Bernard presents them. Not only do we pass from humility to love, to contemplation, but he says this also, "We pass from being the disciple of the Son to being the friend of the Spirit to being the son of the Father (*Filius facit discipulos, Paraclitus consolatur amicos, Pater exaltat filios*) (#20). That's a little history of the spiritual life in one sentence. The Son makes disciples of us and then the

Spirit consoles us as his friends and the Father exalts us as his sons.

We pass from a central concern for authenticity to a very great emphasis on the role of fraternal charity and then to an ongoing experience of God as mystery. This is a typical monastic history, I think. The first years are spent wanting to be a good monk, wanting to overcome the passions, wanting to be holy—and there is nothing wrong with that. That's Christ as Word and Reason and Truth wanting us to become truthful in our innermost self. We pass from that to a very great emphasis on fraternal charity, and then an ongoing experience of God as mystery—and this is another way of saying that we are living out a heightened awareness of each of the Persons, the divine Persons, one by one.

Another Spencer story: at Spencer they pray Terce at the different workplaces. I think a number of monasteries do that, and there is a story that one day an old lay brother was asked to lead Terce; he wasn't accustomed to leading. It came time to begin the Our Father. He was to say the first half and then the community would enter in. So he began, "Our Father who art in heaven, heaven, heaven, heaven" and somebody had to give him a good elbow to get onto the next phrase, because at that moment he too was in heaven. That's the old monk; the basic contact is an ongoing experience of God as mystery.

Putting it in another way, we can see that at different stages we occupy distinct chambers of our inner world. As young adults we try to understand ourselves. We try to figure out our world, to become something in it and find our place in it. Everything is a subject for reflection and comprehension. Later we live in our relationships. We feel that we've really grasped something or someone when we sense an instinctive sympathy with them, and even in the monastery it is usually the members of the middle generation that feel the call to maintain community, to transcend themselves for the others around them. The younger are in the process of being sanctified, the older are in another place. It is the people who have been in the monastery ten, fifteen, twenty years that are building community.

Finally we live in our memory, not in a multitude of recollections but in the continual simplicity of an ongoing awareness of God and his goodness. We sense that this consciousness is just as much heaven as it is earth and that for us, life hidden in God, whether in the here and now or in the hereafter, is our home. And Saint Bernard says that in this stage, whenever we are not enraptured (the majority of the time), the conviction of our sinfulness remains in the reason, but without producing fear. Our compassion for the neighbor perdures in the will, but now without stimulating anxiety. What characterizes the monastic ancient above all is his or her unified *memoria*. It's not that we are a rocket and that different pieces fall off as we ascend: we solve the issues of reason and that falls off and then we move on to love and that falls off and then we are simply contemplation. No. But what happens is that every successive stage purifies the stage immediately prior to it, and so the end picture is very beautiful. Sinful—yes we are, there's no denying it. That is the conviction of the reason, but it is a conviction absolutely without fear, because perfect love casts out fear. Compassion for the neighbor in the will—yes, of course. But without anxiety, because contemplation casts out anxiety. And so finally what really most dominates in the older monk or nun is this *memoria*, this constant consciousness of God. Cassian talks about monastic spiritual maturity as the epoch when all of the monk's words, thoughts, feelings and desires aim at God. Saint Bernard would say that this is the fruit of the unified memory, a memory which the Father has raised up to himself.

Conference 8

The Error of "Self-Abandonment"

If you know *The Divine Comedy* by Dante, if you made it through the first Canto (there are one hundred, but making it through even one counts for something), if you have made it through the first introductory Canto you recall that wonderful introduction where he says, "In the midst of life I found myself lost in the middle of a dark wood." Evidently what he wants to do is to get out of being lost, not to get lost but to get beyond being lost. He spies a hill from a distance, and on the top of the hill is a cross. The sunlight irradiates the hill. It would be nice to go there out of the dark wood into the sunlight, Dante thinks, and the way to do it would be to climb upward—but he cannot. There are three beasts that block his path. The beasts are a symbolical representation of what we call the passions, and there is simply no way beyond them. Every time he tries to advance they push him back, and he thinks that he is going to be stuck forever in the dark wood. It is at that point Virgil appears and lets Dante know that there is one direction that he hasn't looked at in the possible exits from the dark wood, and that is down. The way up is down! We all know this from the Rule of Saint Benedict. It's only by descending within himself that he can get out of the wood, because the nine circles of hell that Dante will be travelling through accompanied by Virgil, who is a symbol of the reason, are cosmic, but they are microcosmic also. They are outside of Dante, they are bigger than Dante. They include all the Florence of his time but they are himself also, and only by dwelling perseveringly in himself (here I am making the shift to Saint Bernard) and coming

89

to something like self despair, can one succeed in escaping from the iron circle of self and entering into communion. It is very mysterious: to get beyond yourself you have to stay within yourself. Not only the way up is down but the way out is in. If you want to get into communion with others you have to go to the very center of yourself. That's where the door is that leads outward. If you know a wonderful commentary by Bruno Barnhart on Saint John's Gospel, *The Good Wine*, he says that John is the most interior and the most exterior of the evangelists. There you find the greatest motion inward and the greatest motion outward. So it is by dwelling within himself and by coming to know his poverty—accepting the fact that every human person is a fraud including himself—that the monk succeeds finally in escaping from the iron circle of self and entering into communion. What happens to the person who gives up on the idea of dwelling with himself, that *habitare secum*? All of us are aware of the first negative commandment that God gave Adam and Eve: not to eat of the tree of the knowledge of good and evil. Perhaps, however, we have forgotten the first positive precept. Saint Bernard brings it up a number of times. "The Lord God placed man and woman in the garden *to till it and cultivate it.*" This was a commandment according to Saint Bernard. There was a purpose for which God placed humanity in the garden. It wasn't just to prance around. There was work to be done, and the work was to take care of the garden. For Saint Bernard this pre-fall commandment is of decisive importance. The garden is our own heart, and our fundamental task is to care for it. All our senses should be turned inward, mounting guard over our heart. "Let all of your senses watch over yourself. Watch over that place in you from which life proceeds, and guard it" *(omnes videlicet sensus tui vigilent ad id unde vita procedit custodiendum)* (#28). This is a reference to Proverbs: "Keep watch over your own heart; for it is from there that life proceeds."

If you are interested in this theme, remember I said I became aware that the Cistercian Fathers, and Saint Bernard in particular, had a doctrine about *nepsis*. I wrote an article about it for *Word and Spirit*. (I believe they are not printing it anymore, it was from

Petersham.) It was the 1990 issue and was all about Saint Bernard. It was a commemorative issue for the centenary of his birth. The article was called, "Custody of the Heart in the *De Diversis* Sermons of Saint Bernard." The intention of the article was to identify the doctrine of the Cistercian Fathers about interior vigilance. So the garden where God placed us is our heart and our job is to watch over it. It is a constant task which will last as long as our life does; it is the only way that purity of heart can be acquired and preserved. It is, says Saint Bernard, our fundamental work in this life; in eternal life, the absorption in God will be such that there will be no need to consciously pay attention to our heart. "If you keep this commandment, when you pass on to better things there will be no need for you either to occupy yourself in any work whatsoever or to exercise this custody." (*Si iniunctum perfeceris, quandoque transitura ad melius, ubi nec opus sit te in aliquo opere occupari, nec de custodia sollicitari*) (#30).

Thus Saint Bernard stands within the classical monastic tradition of *nepsis*, and also the Evagrian tradition which asserts that original sin was a consequence of *negligence* as much as of disobedience: there was a gap in man's dwelling within himself. Obviously this dwelling within oneself is also looking at God. It is not looking at oneself; it is keeping the attention inwardly. From there God raises it to himself, so it is not navel gazing. It is contemplation, but that contemplation requires inward attentiveness. Evagrius affirmed that original sin happened because humanity got tired of, experienced boredom with, the Beatific Vision. It is hard to see how that could be the case but that is what it was according to him. And that was disobedience in the light of this first commandment: to till the garden and to cultivate it.

To be a spiritual creature, as we are and the angels are, is to receive a responsibility to persevere in one's spiritual identity by a constant awareness of it and a constant fidelity to it. When we look outside ourselves without retaining the inward recollection of who we are, we run the risk of acting contrary to our nature or of letting the evil one slip into that central place of our heart and there exert an influence. We joke a lot today, at least we did when I was a young monk, about things like custody of the eyes, but custody of the eyes is not a silly practice that has nothing to do with anything; it is a practice that is contextualized completely within this notion of custody of the heart. Custody of the senses is a first step toward really being able to live in union with your own heart. It's not just an ascetical practice; it's an essential contemplative activity. It is not the deepest part of it but it is an aspect of it.

When the person does not dwell within his own heart by being attentive, when this activity is not practiced, or practiced "half-heartedly" (*torpescit*), the monk is lured outside of himself, into extroversion. For Bernard, the two stances are mutually exclusive: the one who pays attention to himself will not wander outward (*vagari*). He uses the word *vagari*, which does not mean just a momentary slip; it is to live in a state of dispersion and distraction. The one who pays attention to himself will not wander outward, the gaze will rise to God, but the one who ceases to pay complete attention will inevitably look for stimulation elsewhere. "And truly, O man," says Bernard, "if you looked at yourself vigilantly it would be very strange if you found a need to pay attention to anything else." (*Et vere si te vigilanter, homo, attendas, mirum est si aliud umquam attendas*) (# 28). This is that inner paradise which we are; ultimately we are a garden. We are Eden, we are where God dwells and if we pay attention to that, we won't feel the need for television or many other things. But if we don't keep that gaze directed we will wander. I mentioned on the first day that as a good pastor Saint Bernard immediately gives two exceptions to this rule, the two occasions when it is licit, and even praiseworthy, to look outside oneself: when one is in need of spiritual help, or when one's spiritual help is required. Outside of this, all relinquishment of *cura* produces *curiositas*. So *cura* is that care of one's heart, watchfulness over one's heart, and the person who does not practice that *cura* falls into *curiositas*, and *curiositas* is the beginning of pride, and very important for Bernard.

At first glance curiosity seems to be an imperfection and not a sin. After all even in Saint Bernard's own catalog it is only a slackening off as regards the final degree of perfect humility. Remember, if you set up the two ladders, the twelfth degree of humility is perfect humility. When you look at those two ladders the highest degree of humility is standing before God as a sinner, knowing that you are not worthy of eternal life, but that this is going to be granted through the grace of God. In the second ladder (the first one stood on its head), curiosity appears as the first step of pride. Well, we think, curiosity can't be all that bad if it is only the first step of pride. Our temptation is to regard it as nothing particularly serious. But as a matter of fact it is, and for this reason, Bernard shows by means of three biblical figures the dire spiritual consequences that inattentiveness which always leads to curiosity can have.

The first figure is Dinah. She's a very minor figure in the Bible. She was the only daughter of Jacob. He had twelve sons and one daughter. She lived a very enclosed life, as women must have in those times. She was meant to stay inside the tent, and she represents the initial and perhaps the least culpable form of *curiosity*: curiosity of the memory. Remember the union with God of the three faculties, and how it generates humility, charity and contemplation. Now we will see how one by one in the proud person the faculties wander off from God, and here Dinah is the memory wandering off. She's simply thoughtless. She's forgetful of looking after herself. Wants to see what the big wide world is about. The tent which is herself, which is the garden, is not big enough for her, and she knows her brothers get to go out—why shouldn't she too? So she goes out to see the flocks of the pagans in whose midst Jacob's family dwells. It must be interesting. What's a pagan? She'd never seen a pagan, so she wants to see the flocks of the pagans. Possibly there is a link in Saint Bernard's mind, though he does not make it explicit, to that famous verse in the Canticle, "If you do not know who you are, most beautiful of women, go out and see the flocks of your neighbor." So she goes out to see the pagan flocks and what happens? One of the pagans rapes her and she loses her virginity. Precisely, says Saint Bernard. Even when it is only a question of losing our spiritual focus, our concentration, our attention, the consequence will be a loss of our interior virginity. If you let your mind wander, if you give up this practice of inner watchfulness, you don't stay the same. Your reactions are different. Your face is different. Some of you know Brother Gabriel of Spencer; he was the person that entered after me in the community. It was wonderful to live the first year with him. It was like a slow-motion movie; month by month his face changed. His eyes became filled with prayer, the eyes of a man focussed more inwardly than outwardly. I was privileged to see that process take place, and that was because of *my* inattentiveness! So for the person who makes the decision by negligence not to watch over his own heart anymore, gradually that inner virginity will be lost, and for Saint Bernard, the rape of Dinah by the Canaanites is the symbol of that. One "pagan" after another will capture our attention and we will come to live in dispersion, our mind no longer adhering to God as it did before.

The second figure is Eve. Eve symbolizes the curiosity of the *will*; it's a fuller and more serious alienation from the task of inner integrity. One of the things that has moved me most about working with this group is that there is a very clear interest in the life of interior prayer. When you, Brother Placid, mentioned Mark the Ascetic, I nearly fell off my chair. I said, "Well, a junior professed interested in Mark the Ascetic." That did my heart a world of good. When you read many authors about inward prayer they tell you that distractions are of little importance except when you let your will follow the distraction. This is the teaching of Teresa of Avila, for example. One of her images is to call the imagination the fool of the castle who runs around making gestures and noises. But if you don't let your will get caught up in that you can say, "So what?" You really are still in contemplative prayer. The problem is when the will follows after the memory. For Saint Bernard, it is clear that the situation become much more critical when the will abandons this inner attention. This is what happens with Eve. Initially, like Dinah, Eve is "just looking," and she makes it clear in Bernard's text that to her there is nothing wrong in that. She defends herself by saying, "Looking at the apple is not eating it. I'm just looking, I haven't done anything wrong." Saint Bernard says, "Well, yes it is; it *is* eating it. It is the first step in eating the apple." He says, "Even if it is not sin in the full sense of the word it is the occasion of sin. It is the sign of a sin that has

already been committed, and it is the cause of another that is
going to be committed" (*Etsi culpa non est, culpæ tamen occasio est,
et indicium commissæ et causa est committendæ*) (# 30). What is the
sin that has already been committed? The failure to be looking
at the ground you should be tilling. If the person is looking at
the apple then the person is no longer looking inwardly. More
important, "looking" is not a self-contained process. Being who
we are, *attention* habitually generates *desire*. I think it is in the
Rule of Saint Augustine where it says: "Brothers, you're in the
city and you are going off to market and you see a beautiful
woman. That's no problem. Where the problem is, is looking
more than once. There is no problem in looking once, but if you
look twice you're in trouble. Looking once is something that just
happens. You're on the way to market and there she is. What you
could do? God put her in your path. She has presented herself
to your gaze. Fine, keep going to market. But if once she passes,
you deliberately fix your attention on her, that's not going to stay
attention; it is going to become desire." Repeated active attention
generates desire, and this is what happened with Eve. She didn't
just see the apple; she kept looking at the apple. When the attention is wrongly placed, the desire that it generates is *concupiscence*.
Eve deceives herself when she asserts that curiosity can remain
at the level of misguided attention. We know that for the advanced monastics it can be helpful to let themselves be tempted.
Remember, this is for advanced monks and nuns. When something tempts us, and we already have a certain amount of self
dominion, we should let that temptation play itself out as if it
were a movie, because we will learn a lot about ourselves. We
could get to know the roots of what the problem is and why it is
that this object exercises so much attraction or creates so much
irritation or depresses us. But that's not for beginners. If beginners experience one of the passions, their job is to cut it off immediately, because if they keep looking at it, with the lack of self
dominion that they have, they will end up like Brer Rabbit with
the tar baby. Brer Rabbit starts out by having one hand in the tar
baby, and maybe he could have gotten himself free of it if he had
only stayed on the level of one hand. But then he hits the tar baby

with the other hand because he is mad at it, and he is stuck with both hands. Then he kicks it with one foot and he kicks it with the other foot and there he is completely caught without a hope in the world of deliverance. So, for us beginners in the spiritual life, as soon as we feel one of the passions, we should do what Saint Benedict says we should do, we should dash it against the rock which is Christ. As to people further along, the desert tradition is very clear. It can be very helpful to just watch, because you watch without being involved passionately. You are simply there, you're seeing it. Along with being fascinating it is very instructive, but not at the start of the spiritual life. Eve deceived herself when she asserted that curiosity could just be curiosity. Curiosity for the beginner always transmutes into desire. Without a real battle to regain correct focus, curiosity leads to an attachment of the will, and thence to a choice that contradicts our conscience and the commandment of God. This curiosity of the will is deadly, because it provokes a decision to disobey the will of God. The two wills are now in conflict, ours and God's. And so, says Saint Bernard, "Eve's curiosity has proved deadly both for herself and for all her descendants."

The final figure in this series of portraits of curiosity is Lucifer. His importance is such that we will dedicate an entire conference to him. Certainly, this will flatter his pride! Who was it who said, "I don't care if they are talking well or ill of me as long as they are talking about me"? The opposite story is the story about Eleanor Roosevelt who as a teenager once said, "Papa, why is it that people are always thinking bad things about me?" His reply was, "Eleanor, my dear, people are not thinking bad things about you. They are not thinking about you. They are thinking about themselves." Lucifer represents the ultimate curiosity, curiosity of the *reason*. Initially Lucifer has let his attention wander from himself, from his vigilance, to God's throne. Saint Bernard says, "He looks up to the North," *ex obliquo (ex obliquo intendis ad aquilonem)* (#31). We would say: out of the corner of his eye. He just wants to see what that throne is like. It is beautiful. From memory it goes on to will. He sets his will on attaining equality with God. But how does he imagine that such a thing can be possible, that

God will enable him to set himself up as co-God on an adjoining throne? Where did he ever get that idea? Such a thought is only possible to someone who has allowed his reason to stray from himself, who instead of really thinking, gets involved in *machinations*. His reason has been perverted by his desire. He so much wants to sit on the second throne equal to that of God that it affects his thinking. He keeps reformulating the truth in his inner reflections until he manages to conform it to his desire. Lucifer comes to feel that his autodivinization is not only possible but *secure*. "I can do it and God will not be able to deprive me of it." The punishment of this alienation from truth is eternal alienation and nonbelonging. Lucifer ends up as the "eternal vagrant." He was not happy in his place. He wanted another place that did not belong to him, and he ends up living no place. Saint Bernard says that Lucifer is the eternal vagrant, and he lives feeling the eternal punishment of his own fluctuation (*pœnam sentias propriæ fluctuationis*) (#34). He has abandoned his seat and wished for the only one that was too high for him, and therefore he has no place anymore, hovering between heaven and earth, the "prince of the power of the air."

The three curiosities, as well as being seen in terms of the faculties, can be seen in terms of their objects. Dinah's is a curiosity that has to do with *experience*: unsatisfied with what she finds in her father's house, she wants to see and hear what goes on in the tents of the alien neighbors. There is a book by John Dunne, *A Search for God in Time and Memory*. It's an interesting book on Saint Augustine, and he says that Saint Augustine was an "experience junkie." He wanted to do everything, and he wanted to have the experience of everything. Faust is another case of that, he wants to experience everything. That's why he makes a pact with the devil. He's an old man and he knows everything. He starts with a wonderful soliloquy: "I've studied chemistry, I've studied history, I've studied philosophy, and I've studied alchemy," and I think he concludes, "and unfortunately I have also studied theology." But then the devil comes to him and says, "Listen, maybe you *know* it all, but you haven't *done* it all and this will be our pact: if you will sell your soul to me, you will be a handsome young man and I will take you wherever you want, to do whatever you want with whomever you want in all the corners of the globe for as long as you live." He couldn't resist the pact. His curiosity, too, is a curiosity of experience. Karl Rahner, in one of his articles in *Theological Investigations*, written in the fifties (reading it now, we might think it was written just yesterday), said that we live in a situation where the banquet of life placed in front of us is very rich, but we starve because we cannot make a choice. There are so many choices and everything looks so good that we never put anything on a plate because we want it all, and we want the best of it all, and we end up with very little. This is curiosity of experience. A very home grown example of the same thing is Dorothy. Dorothy, who can't be satisfied with Kansas, goes to Oz. And remember she says that it was a very interesting place with a lot of beautiful things, but there were a lot of horrible things as well, and her great lesson is when she clicks her heels three times and says, "There's no place like home." Saint Bernard would be delighted with that, because home is where the heart is, and the heart is where home is. Very frequently at Novo Mundo, when a person is about to make first vows they'll send me a note. They don't realize that they are doing it one after the other, all quoting the same verse of Psalm 132: "This is my resting place forever; here will I dwell." It is the discovery of a home that satisfies. No more need to wander, no more desire for other experiences. I had a lovely experience of that Monday night last week when Father Michael picked me up at the airport at Gethsemani and he said, "Now what would you like to see while you are here? There is My Old Kentucky Home; there is the Bardstown Cathedral." I said, "I would like to spend two days in Gethsemani with the brethren." That's a blessing of aging I think. The curiosity for new experiences diminishes.

Dinah's is thus a curiosity of experience. Dinah was just a kid. Had she been older the pagans would not have wanted her. Eve's is a curiosity of *knowledge*; it is intellectual curiosity, in the negative sense of the term. It is given to her to know all that is good, but she cannot rest until she has had the knowledge of evil as well.

By the way, Father Elias* wrote in *Cistercian Studies Quarterly* a study on a very brief sermon of Saint Bernard: not the five ways of knowing but the five motives of knowing, which is very interesting for monks. There are five motivations for knowing. The first is curiosity. The second is to show off. The third is to make a profit—are you going to sell your knowledge to live off it? The fourth is to know God, and the fifth is to serve your neighbor. Eve's was the first: the curiosity of knowledge. She wants to know experientially. She wants to know what evil is. And Saint Bernard tells her, "Eve, you're wrong. To know evil is not to know, but to become a fool. Sometimes Saint Bernard is untranslatable. "To be wise in evil is not wisdom but foolishness." The problem is that the word to be *wise* is also the word to *taste*. So he's making a pun about the apple and the experience of tasting the apple, and so he says, "To know evil, that is to say, to taste evil is not to taste, but to become foolish" (*Sapere enim malum, sapere non est, sed desipere*) (# 30). The verb *desipere* also means to become tasteless. You lose your own flavor; to taste evil is to become a person that has no flavor (which of course is what happens to Eve in eating the fruit against God's will). So Dinah's curiosity is of *experience*, Eve's of *knowledge*, Lucifer's is an *ontological* curiosity. He desires to be other than he is, different than he is, more than he is. He finds a way to justify the thought that he should be this more and he can be this more (distortion of the reason by desire).

Curiosity is the result of losing one's grip on the blessing of one's own spiritual identity. For Dinah blessedness was to live in her father's house; for Eve, the blessing was to live in paradise. "Eve," says Saint Bernard, "how could you do this? You have been placed in paradise" (*in paradiso posita es*) (#30). In the case of Lucifer, he had experienced the utmost delights of paradise. "You were placed *in deliciis paradisi*; it doesn't get better than that, Lucifer. How could you have been so stupid? Really, to have decided to rebel against God you had to have gone temporarily

---

* Dom Elias Dietz, current abbot of Gethsemani Abbey, Kentucky. Ed.

insane. You have to have lost your reason, because you were in the best place imaginable."

What happens when we lose the blessing of our own spiritual identity? It is not so easily recoverable. Remember, Saint Bernard says you have to go through the punishment of humility, and not everybody is ready for punishment. (Saint Ignatius in his *Constitutions* says—I'm paraphrasing—"Never correct a person immediately after they have sinned. The fact that they have sinned shows you that they're not in the mood for virtue. If you are going to correct them immediately after they have sinned, be prepared for a smart-alecky answer because that is the spiritual stance they are in.") These biblical characters sin by inattentiveness and for the time being they are deprived of their blessedness, their genuine spiritual identity. Dissatisfaction automatically sets in, and they go out of themselves trying to recuperate *outside* what they have left behind *inside*. That is a further step of curiosity. They think that they can just take a quick look on the outside, get something from the outside and bring it in, only to find they are in exile from themselves. When they try to get back in, they find that the door has been shut. The curious person goes out of himself trying to recuperate outside what he had left behind inside. This is the essence of the tragedy of the proud person. Unaware previously of the genuine blessedness of his identity which requires nothing additional, only to persevere in it, the curious person goes out of himself and encounters a world of objects and persons, and immediately this sets off a reaction. These objects and persons are not neutral; they either promise his completion or seem to threaten it. Because this person has lost contact with himself, he goes out into the world of extroversion and *needs* that world to complete the now incomplete self. He will be very wary about what objects seem to complete him and what objects seem to threaten the remainder of what he has left. Everything will be looked at from that angle—especially persons. Someone whose thing is intellectual excellence, if that person becomes curious, the first thing that he does when he goes into a room will be to look around to see if there's anyone there smarter than he is. That will be an instinctive reaction in the person who has lost that peaceful stable contact with himself. Life becomes instantaneously comparative and immediately there will be an evaluation. Who is better; who is worse? The person who goes out of himself needs the world to complete him and has that evaluative glance. He thinks he can perfect himself either by acquiring what he discovers in the outside world that can help him or eliminating it if it seems to threaten him. The harder he tries, the more he wanders from himself, and sadly, the more he will fail. The more he tries to make up for his lost blessedness by using the world to build himself up, the further away he gets from himself. The conclusion is that the curious person ends up without his soul *and* without the world for which he sold it. It's a reformulation of the great saying of Jesus, and now it reads: "What does it profit a man to lose the whole world *and* his own soul?" That's what begins to happen to a person when he runs away from himself and goes into the world of curiosity.

Conference 9

Pride as the Destruction of Relationship

Right at the beginning of his treatise, immediately after giving us a synoptic look at the two ladders of pride and humility, Saint Bernard describes the trajectory of pride in terms of the severing of genuine relationship. The first six steps of the ladder of pride involve contempt of one's brethren; the next four, contempt of the abbot; the last two, contempt of God himself.

We have seen how the monk, through negligence or unresolved anxiety, abandons himself by abandoning the guardianship of the heart: *custodia cordis*. Henceforth, everything he does will be aimed at recuperating the lost glory of being himself in himself and in God. But he will be running in the wrong direction.

This direction will consist in the *insistence on his own specialness*. It is important to interpret correctly this Bernadine definition of pride—that pride is the love of one's own excellence, *amor propriæ excellentiæ*. First of all this "love" is not disinterested aesthetic appreciation. There would be a way that you could look at yourself and rejoice. You think of Psalm 8, that God has set the human person above all the creatures—the birds of the air, the fish of the sea and all that crawls on the earth—he has given all things into mankind's hands. To glory in that, theologically, is not pride. It is praise. Or there is a beautiful passage in Sophocles which speaks of all of the marvels that the gods have created, and it goes through a tremendous list of them, and finally comes to the greatest marvel of all, which is a human person. That's the Bible, it is Sophocles but also the Bible, that is why man is made on the last day. He is the apex of creation. God saved the best for last.

But that is not what this love of one's own excellence means. It is not a looking at oneself and rejoicing in oneself and giving praise to the one from whom one came. It is dogged self-centered commitment. More important is the recognition that, in its original meaning, excellence is a comparative term. Excellence doesn't mean good, it means better than, the best of the particular group, it means to excel, *excellentia*. What the proud person loves is not to be peacefully good (that he had before when he dwelt in himself) but to be shiningly *better* than others. That's the new goal. Interestingly he was better off when he was self-centered. It seems like a paradox, but when he was peacefully at home in himself there wasn't this hostility, there wasn't this competitiveness. Now he has to outdo the others.

And here we have the basic problem of pride. When the human person leaves the paradise of living with himself, *habitare secum*, he immediately divides humanity, says Saint Bernard, into two categories that are based on his ego and his ego needs: persons superior to himself and persons inferior to himself. It's an immediate classification that goes on in the case of the proud person. I catalog and I separate. For the interior person, everyone is "in the same boat"; the exteriorized person is divided from everyone, and likewise divides everyone into these two groups of superiors (*superiores*) and inferiors (*inferiores*). This means that for the proud person, totally concentrated on confirming his specialness, other persons really don't exist as persons. They are around simply to shore him up, to tell him that he is better than they are. That's why other people exist, to be lesser and by being lesser to affirm me. The proud person is constantly working toward this, and working to have other people actually acclaim him as being superior to themselves. Temporarily, according to Saint Bernard, he may succeed in doing this in the sixth degree of pride, which is arrogance. All of the interaction of the proud person with his peers revolves around this effort to believe himself interiorly superior to all. This can coexist with being very polite, very decent and very friendly. At some point of my own career at Spencer I thought about the people in community that I had difficulty with and I asked myself: Where is the difficulty on my end? I must be giving a message without a word, without a gesture, with perfect elegance and yet unconsciously, I must be saying something. And I found it. I kept asking God to tell me what it was that I was saying, and I was saying to them, "You're not a real monk." That was the message I was communicating, which means I am a better monk than you are. I am not sure if the recipients were *conscious* of the message—but they got the message. I'm not sure if the message flashed across the screen in legible terms, but it was received, and it was that message which created the barrier. And interestingly, the proud person conceals that from himself. Actually he has a very different feeling; he has a feeling that he's being lovely and fraternal. Look how he goes out to all the brethren and is kind and attentive to them all, unaware that there is this subliminal message which both of them are reading. He's happy about it also, but I think the happiness is fairly well hidden. He misinterprets the source of his happiness. He thinks he's happy because he's being a good brother, and the real happiness is that he's being a *better* brother. So all of the interactions of the proud person, the proud monk, with his peers have this one goal: to feel better than the others. This certainly does constitute a *contemptus fratrum*, contempt of the brothers—and actually for the proud monk "brothers" is an ironic term, since the rest of the community does not mean anything to him apart from the glory they can offer him. When I was a novice, I used to have these one-minute, humiliating visions that God sent me, the only kind that I really needed. Once I saw myself on a stage with everyone in Spencer around me, and me with the microphone. It was like Diana Ross and the Supremes, and my job was to sing the solo and the community's job was to sing, "doo wah, doo wah." So they are the backup group. The community becomes your backup group, your family becomes your backup group. It is a horrible way of thinking about them. When Saint Bernard says it is a love of being special he is really talking about love; it is what the person loves. It is the object of his love—being special, and so this means that everybody else has to fit into that project and be subsumed into it. So on the one hand, the brethren don't mean anything. They are purely instrumental and yet paradoxically, says Saint Bernard, on the other hand the brethren mean too much. The proud monk is always measuring himself against others, is always forming his ideas of himself based on others, and ultimately he goes so far as to ask the brothers to tell him who he is. It is really quite strange: he despises them and yet he is always asking them to tell him how good he is, because he can't believe it about himself. "The very person who on every other subject trusts more in himself than in others, when it comes to himself, trusts what others say more than what he himself thinks." *(Quique de omni alia re plus sibi credit quam aliis, de se solo plus aliis credit quam sibi)* (#43). It may not be logical, but enough of us have experienced it firsthand to know that it is the case. The proud person needs that constant affirmation from the outside, and yet the appearance that he gives is that he needs nothing from anyone.

In response to a question about the proud person's need for affirmation:

The proud monk has a love of being special but he doesn't have a security about it, he never feels completely sure that he really is special, so he needs to do things that will constantly say it again and again to him: "You're special." One very primitive way of seeming to be special is to insist on being the focus of attention. You're the one who is talking, you're the one who is singing, you're the one who is telling a joke, you're the one who won an award, you're the one that's giving an opinion. And other people, very often unwillingly, are forced into being just listeners, or are paying attention out of politeness. But that kind of person is very needy, because he loves the specialness and yet he doubts the specialness. What frees him from doubt, at least for the moment, is the attention, the smiles of the others. They say (I'm not sure if this is true or not) that the comedian is the great insecure one, because every time people laugh, he is given back his identity. He doesn't feel that he's anybody except when he's on stage and telling one joke after another, and people laugh and he interprets that laugh as a mixture of admiration and love. But really, we can never derive our identity from the applause of other people. It's a losing game and that's why the person can never say that's enough; he will always need more.

In response to a question about what can free one from the need to be extraordinary:

I think that to some extent the power to change comes from an intuition into what is actually going on. Remember I spoke yesterday of that class when I tried to take the authority away from the professor. I was having a hell of a time until I realized what I was doing, and then I felt physically nauseous. When I saw that it was a very egocentric bid to put myself on a pedestal above the professor, have everyone think of me as the great intellectual, let that be known for now and all time, I said, Oh, my God, that is not only humiliating but morally it's horrible. That poor professor—I am amazed he didn't tell me to shut up at some point, and he didn't. What shut me up was the intuition. I'm amazed that the other novices didn't say, "Give it a rest," which they should have. I myself am not so patient. When I give classes, if there is a novice who predominates, predominates, predominates, after a few classes I call him aside and I say, "Let's think about what you're doing and what it is you're doing to the people in the class and what it is you are doing to the communication in the class." It's painful, but it can help, it is an intuition into the truth. I think that's basically what Saint Bernard is saying: what can heal us from these patterns is the truth. That passage we heard yesterday or the day before from the Apocalypse, "You say, 'I am rich, I have everything that I need,' whereas the truth is you are naked and blind and poor." When you get involved in these behaviors of needing attention or whatever it might be, it has an illusory side to it, and I think Saint Bernard is saying that when Christ illumines you, you see what it is that you're going after. And also, how instead of elevating yourself you're pandering to yourself, you're selling yourself. And that's a big help toward stopping. I think before you have the intuition of what is going on, you don't have a sufficient reason to stop, but if you can see it for what it is, I think that can help.

I don't know how many of you would have heard of Karen Horney, that great psychoanalyst who worked in New York. She has a very important book called *Neurosis and Human Growth*, and she speaks a lot about these same themes: this uneasy linking between an outward assertion of superiority and a constant anxiety about one's standing in relation to others because one does not stand in one's own reality, this veering back and forth between being outwardly secure and inwardly self-doubting. According to her it is the hallmark of the neurotic. It is very close to Saint Bernard. She says the neurotic abandons the realistic grasp on himself, and once that happens he oscillates between what she calls self-inflation, which in order to function has to include contempt of others, and self-deflation, which is doubt, contempt about oneself. She says that it is a terrible condemnation because one lives painfully passing back and forth between attempts to make oneself seem tremendous (and this by stepping on the shoulders of others) and the inevitable recoil, and the recoil is a very deep doubt about whether you are worth anything at all. Because the person has become uncentered. If we are centered in ourselves, she says, we are simply in our assigned orbit. There is a self-sameness to it, there is a healthy consistency to it, which is lost once we've abandoned who we are for some vision of glory. For her, glory is the goal of the neurotic. She speaks very frequently about neurotic glory, which is a desire to affirm yourself publicly as something more than what you are—to such an extent that you sell your soul. That's the term she uses. And insofar as you sell your soul for neurotic glory you are condemned to this very painful alternation. It would really be interesting to see a comparative study done of these two authors. I don't think she knew the works of Saint Bernard, but she makes frequent use of literary models in her works, so certainly it would be interesting to her.

Saint Bernard masterfully traces out the efforts of the proud monk to entrench himself in this position of superiority. The process begins by a twofold tactic, *repression* and *exaggeration*. The monk diminishes to an absolute minimum in his mind the gifts and talents of others and augments their defects. We do it all the time. We just redimension the person. If you look at the person objectively, you see that they have their abilities and gifts. But when you look through your special telescope those gifts become smaller and the defects become bigger. So you relativize all of the good aspects of the person, and you universalize, aggrandize, all of the negative aspects of the person. That's what you do with others; with regards to yourself it is the opposite. There is not a single person here who didn't go through a stage (and maybe it's still going on), where he says about himself: "I am a hell of a nice guy." I just recently had a conversation with one of the most violent persons I know who said to me, "You know, so many people in this world are people of war: me, I am a love person." I thought to myself, "Yes, that is news!" But that is a myth that the person created about himself: I am a love person. "Could you give me an example?" I wanted to say to him. It's that same telescope turned one way when it is directed toward ourselves, and turned the other way when directed to another person. It is the "yes, but." *Yes*, Placid has this talent, this talent, this talent, *but*—and the "but" will somehow obliterate all the other stuff. Those talents don't really matter because he has this flaw, and that's just the kind of flaw that makes mince meat of his many other qualities. Whereas in my own case I might be loud and boisterous and this and that and the other thing, but underneath these baggy pants there beats a heart of gold.

In regard to a question about psychological attitudes formed in childhood:

Yes, that's a problem. Saint Bernard doesn't reflect on that; I don't think he took that into account. These attitudes are being formed from your earliest years, and by the time you're aware of them you are grown up and it is a tremendous job to start working on them, and you spend many years in the monastery doing so. For example, when I was three I was very good at arithmetic. My parents would invite neighbors over and put me in a corner so I could concentrate. I would face the wall. They would have calculators. They would give me these multiplications or divisions or subtractions or additions to do in my head as they would do them on the calculator, and they would want me to come out with the answer before the calculator did—and I did! Everyone applauded. I thought I was the cat's meow also, but that is one of the things which begins to establish the pattern in a person of becoming a performer, and a feeling that his value consists in being able to do these extraordinary mental feats, because that makes people happy with you and that's your place in the world. In some form or other, this happens with everybody. Those behaviors won us approbation, but that often involved, almost always, some kind of inauthenticity. Then we grow up and we get a certain light of grace and we see, "Wow, how am I going to get out of this one?" It is not going to be fast, and it probably will never be total.

This year on Ash Wednesday I gave to each of the persons in the community an instrument of good works for their Lenten penance. I've done it over the last five years. Up until this year the texts have always been drawn from the Rule, Chapter 4. This year I said, I'm going for the jugular (I prayed over each one quite a bit, so that it was a nice jugular). In the past, I had asked people to read the text of their instrument out loud, but not this year because sometimes they were really personal. There is one person in the community who is really saintly. He has two basic difficulties that he still fighting with, obstinacy and curiosity. He loves to know everything. The obstinacy I think is something worse, but after praying and praying and praying I decided not to put that on the paper. So I said something about, "Try to keep your attention fixed on Jesus Christ, the goal, and not to be so involved with passing issues that really don't matter." Now that ended up being fairly light in comparison to what other people got. Two days later he was in my office saying, "That's not true." I said, "What's not true?" "That's not true." I said, "Brother, if you want we will talk about it, but first of all that instrument was given to you as an ascetical practice and as a means of conversion, not for you to say that it is not true. If at the end of forty days you believe it's not true come and tell me and I'll be glad to change my mind." But then I said to myself, "Hell, I wish I had put obstinacy!" This person really is a saint; he just has these two little things that he's been working on. They must be from very early on. So monastic life is a task. Working on these things is only part of the monastic life, but a part that will be with us in some way until the end. "And never to despair of God's mercy," as Saint Benedict says.

The proud monk eliminates the superiority of others, which is a source of sadness for him. This is very mysterious. I hope we have all experienced it. To consciously feel sadness at someone else's good fortune or success. When Sister Maureen and I went into the bookshop together, we saw her book on the Psalms. I said, "Why aren't my books of sermons there?" It took me a few days to remember that they are in Portuguese, and Conyers doesn't have books in Portuguese. But my first reaction was, "Well, she's a presenter, so what am I, chopped liver?" That is in all of us, and it will be, until we can become truly humble. So we try to put things into parentheses. Anything that makes the other better, greater, deeper than we are. And we maximize our own positive qualities because they are a source of gladness, but it is a strange kind of gladness because it rests on a willed suppression of the truth. You really have to throw a blanket over the truth to convince yourself that you're better than everybody. Nobody is better than everybody. But even if someone were, it is not going to be us. Who would it be? God knows. In a course that I took on Saint John's Gospel (we were first year theologians) the professor who was a Lebanese Jesuit said, "Listen, guys, there is one genius a century and in the twentieth century, as I read it, it was Proust, so let's forget our self inflation and get on with this." I thought that was very interesting. The genius of the twentieth century. The twenty-first century is still a baby so let's not worry about it now. But you have this monk who is glad because he is better than anyone else, and now he is an overly happy monk. He is overly happy, because it is an exaggeration that is flawed, that is fluff, that is froth, because it is not based on reality; and then he goes about relating with others in conformity with his swollen self-concept. Saint Bernard says this person perpetually bubbles over. He is an unquenchable fountain of knowledge, with common sense and theological insights, and yet at the same time as he speaks he is "selling his image," attempting to prove to himself and his companions that he really "knows it all." Unfortunately, there is never any time or energy left to listen to anybody else. Saint Bernard says this person answers when he has not been asked a question. He himself does the questioning, he himself gives the answer, and if anybody else tries to give an answer he cuts them off in the middle *(Prævenit interrogantem, non quærenti respondet. Ipse quærit, ipse solvit, et verba collocutoris imperfecta præcidit)* (#41). Nor is there really any need to hear them out: other people serve their purpose by being present, listening and nodding their approval: *Esurit et sitit auditores* (#41).

Saint Bernard says that this person has a hunger and thirst for listeners. Blessed are those who hunger and thirst for listeners. You don't have to say anything, just be my audience. How many marriages are built on that, how many friendships? I had a Jesuit friend who would say when we would get together, "Listen, we only have twenty minutes. I'll take the first ten and you take the second ten." No idea of a dialog. Each person would have ten solid minutes of being the absolute focus of attention. He was being ironic when he said it, but it is so very common. What this person does in words he does in actions as well. The brethren in their common life are the backdrop for his starring role. Their place is to manifest the ordinary and in so doing to orient him to the extraordinary. The ordinary for him is despicable since it is what the multitude does. It does however allow him to go one better in everything. To fast more, to pray more, to weep more. Saint Bernard talks about the person who falls asleep at Vespers, but everybody knows he is in the chapel until midnight. Every night on his knees before the Blessed Sacrament. There is a snack here and a snack there and a snack every place else but at the noon time meal there are a couple of grains of rice and a couple of beans and a piece of lettuce and half a glass of water.

(A reflection of mine that has the "ring" of Saint Bernard, though I have never found it in his writings, is that Cain, firstborn son of Eve, gives a special twist to this twofold tendency. The first moment we meet him, we see him considering Abel more acceptable to God because for some unjust reason he has been able to present a superior sacrifice. This is intolerable to Cain, and so he slays his brother. Could it be that Abel's sacrifice was *not* superior after all, that it was simply Abel's, but that Cain in his excessive desire to assert his own specialness and his suspicion regarding anybody else's specialness overvalued Abel's gift, killing him because his brother's gift humiliated him?)

Here's another look at the monk who's a specialist in *singularitas*. He's telling jokes during the grand silence, he is reading the newspaper when he shouldn't be, but at the adoration of the Cross on Good Friday he is inconsolable. Cry, cry, cry, because only he and Jesus know what Jesus went through and maybe even Jesus doesn't! This could be called a Mel Gibson complex. This is the fifth degree of pride, which is to be extraordinary, to be different in everything, and that's why for such a person it's so great to have the brothers around, because they are all ordinary, all living according to the Rule. At lunch time they eat lunch, at Vespers they sing, after Compline they go to sleep. Terrific! The more they stick to that, the more the extraordinary "I" is shown in all of its splendor.

(Another novice story. This was in mental prayer. I was praying and all of a sudden I looked, and there was a statue of gold and on the base of the pedestal were engraved the words "Great Saint Bernard," and I knew that it wasn't Bernard of Clairvaux. That was scene one, a beautiful statue. The second scene: in comes an angel, like the kind in the Don Camillo books. He comes with a sledge hammer, and gives an immense bang to the statue, which immediately falls down and breaks into a million pieces. Scene three: he goes out and comes back with dustpan and a broom, picks up all the pieces and throws them into the trash. Scene four: he comes back again, bows from the waist, and exits. That's the end of the vision. I said, "Wow, monastic life is going to be a killer." Because it was clear right away what it was God was trying to tell me. This great Saint Bernard who is different and better, who was a man of gold, is a fraud. It's a creation of the fantasy, and the angels of God are not going to stand for it, and there will be more joy among the angels of God for destroying that statute than I had in creating it.)

Everything that this person does is now oriented toward this specialness. It becomes absolutely obsessive. He talks, talks, talks on every subject. He has no interest in teaching you, and even less interest in being taught by you that which he already knows. The only thing that he cares about is that you know that he knows what he knows. That's it, it is just a performance; his sole purpose whenever he talks to you is that you go away knowing that he knows. And the same is true with any religious practice. We see that for the proud man, not only do other persons lose their subjectivity; human activities lose their intrinsic worth as well. Knowledge no longer exists as a way to wisdom, but as an opportunity to vaunt oneself (*Non curat te docere vel a te doceri ipse quod nescit, sed ut scire sciatur ut scit*) (#41). Religious practice no longer exists for him as a means to sanctification, but as one more way to grow in the esteem of others (*apud simpliciores eius opinio excreverit* (#42). He particularly cultivates the simpler brothers, those who have less acumen, those who are more likely to be taken in. He goes and gives them a conference, an unasked for conference on this, that, or the other thing. And indeed, says Saint Bernard, for a while his fame grows among the more simple.

The brethren complete the task he has assigned them when they glorify him (*beatificare*), when they ratify the superiority he hungered after. Presumably the brothers feel that in giving due praise to his virtues, they are growing closer in communion with him, but he for his part sees himself permanently lifted above them. It's a kind of ascension he is living.

This initiates his destruction as a monk. Once he's come to this stage, fully convinced at last that he really is better than the rest, he expresses this conviction in haughty interference in all the affairs of the community. For a while the abbot and his authority are acceptable, since they, too, can possibly serve as an ongoing acknowledgment of his own gifts: "Why, once again you're *right*, Br. Melchizedek! I don't think we've had such an intelligent, holy and capable monk in the Order since 1098, the founding of Cîteaux." In other words, the abbot's authority can be subsumed into the monk's project of excellence.

But should the abbot insist on his independent identity and on his role as spiritual guide and disciplinarian—of *this* monk— the situation becomes intolerable. Now the abbot is useless: is he is going to correct *me*? What is he good for? Is he going to treat me like the others who need him? Above all in the case where he calls this monk to interior and exterior conversion. "This would imply that I am a sinner. No; unthinkable." So the abbot has to go, at least as a person who has any authority over me or who enjoys my respect. Although there is one last scene with the abbot. "It could be interesting," says the proud monk, "to go through a false conversion, because this can be played up too. I can be extraordinary in my repentance. I can go to the abbot's room and knock on the abbot's door and be found kneeling there six or seven times a day. 'I'm so sorry, Reverend Father. If I thought that I was hurting you I would never have done that. Can you forgive me?' If the abbot goes along with it, it could be truly delightful. In that case, he's 'in' again. He's *my* abbot."

In response to a question as to what would be the experience of a proud monk listening to this talk:

I would say that Saint Bernard certainly didn't write this book just from observation of other people. This is a mirror of his own soul as well. And so I would say, if you are a proud monk, you're in the monastery of Clairvaux, together with him and all the rest of us. He's trying to give us those insights because he feels that insights can help to change the behaviors, and he is trying to give them in a way that makes us laugh, because the object is not to kill or to dishearten. It is to give the person the courage to turn around and go back again toward the way of humility. And Saint Bernard says this in one of the *De Diversis* sermons: we spend a long time fighting for the enemy, but once we realize that we're on the wrong side of the battle and we start fighting for Christ and for our true self, it doesn't matter that the battle is the same. What matters is that we have changed sides. In other words, we may continue to be egocentric, to claim attention, to be a know it all, to be incapable of admitting our own fallibility. Saint Bernard says, if you no longer wish to do that, because your wish is to be with Christ and for Christ, then everything has changed. Visibly nothing has changed, but in terms of the outcome it is going to be wonderful. This is probably the punishment of humility: to keep on doing these same things for a while, but without wanting to do them and without getting any ego boosts out of them. Before there was a certain element of delight in it all and now there isn't.

In response to a question about the situation of someone who initially says no to God's attempts to bring him to self-knowledge but eventually opens himself to them:

I think that is beautiful, sister. You know why? The Jewish tradition, the tradition Jesus would have known, usually gives things in groups of four, because when you're dealing with two people and two alternatives there are four possible outcomes. So if Jesus had taught in the Talmudic tradition, there would have been four sons. The son who said "yes" and did not go, and the son who said, "no" and went. They are the ones in the gospel. But there would also be the son who said, "yes" and went and then the son who said "no" and didn't go. Why didn't Jesus include those other two sons? It would have filled out the picture logically. Listening to you, I think it is because his intuition is that there is only column A and column B. Until a very great sanctity (or a very great antisanctity) has been established, we are going to be one of the two that Jesus mentions. The other two exist theoretically, but not in real life. So I would agree with you that you shouldn't beat yourself up about having an initial reaction of resistance, and afterward going to do what God asks. That's exactly the son that Christ presents to us as a model.

We were talking about the proud monk being corrected by his abbot. If the abbot, instead of being taken in by the monk, says, "Oh please, you have said you are sorry, I accept your apology. You do have some things that need to be corrected but we will work on them"—well, that's exactly what he doesn't want to hear because that puts him into the community. He's now a monk like everybody else, somebody who most of the time is good but once in a while sins. That is just the message he cannot accept. The abbot has broken the unspoken pact, and from henceforth his authority can only be despised. To genuinely bend before the abbot's correction would be to lose the whole game, to become a nobody. To become like everyone else in the community! That's sad, if being one of the brethren means to be a nobody. That is really tragic, but that's where the monk is at this stage of the ladder of pride.

For the time being the monk is still in relationship with God, even though he despises the brothers and denies the abbot's authority. Saint Bernard says that if things have come to this level, the person has to go; he has to be sent away from the community. It is strong doctrine. So now the monk finds himself outside the monastery. But he is still a Catholic, still a man of the church. Yes, Saint Bernard says, perhaps for a little while, but contempt is *corrosive* and *expansive*. Just as to know the truth of humility about oneself naturally leads to knowing the truth of the other and of God, so too contempt for one's peers carries within it the fundamental components for contempt of authority and contempt of God. You know the saying of the desert fathers where a brother makes a depreciative remark about another brother and the brother to whom he is speaking says, "Don't say that. If you speak badly about your brother, you might end up speaking badly about the monastic council." And the guy then says, "Well, I don't think that much of the monastic council either; they are not perfect, you know." The second brother says, "Well, don't say that. You could end up speaking badly about the abbot." "Well, I am not really in love with the abbot either. He is not the one I voted for. I think he's doing a decent job but it is not so great. It could be done better." "Well, don't speak like because you could end up talking badly about the Bishop." "That Bishop! You want to hear what I think about that Bishop?" And on goes the story to its terrifying end when the monk bad mouths the Blessed Trinity. It's the same idea as in Saint Bernard, that contempt is corrosive and expansive. Once you begin to despise anybody you are on your way to despising everybody, human and divine. Contempt distorts all relationships. It makes us instrumentalize the brethren into a flattering contrast with ourselves; it makes us reformulate abbatial authority into an instrument of our public recognition. And now it makes us consider God merely as *power*, power to be tested to see whether it may be successfully thwarted. In the eleventh degree of pride, the monk becomes a habitual sinner. He breaks God's laws because he wants to, and because he wants to see what he can get away with. He elbows God to see if God is going to elbow him back or if nothing is going to happen. He dabbles in sin and then immerses himself in it. For a while he keeps his eye on God to see whether any punishment will be forthcoming. Once he establishes experientially that sin is not followed immediately by punishment, God loses all interest for him and he says, "Well, at least the abbot punishes once in a while but God doesn't do a thing. I don't have to worry about him." Up to now, God "cramped his style," put some limits on his plan to have no limits. And now he thinks he sees that God as moral authority is impotent, and that he himself has complete scope to do whatever he wants. Chillingly, the proud monk in the thoughts of his heart has come very close to Nietzsche.

Saint Bernard, talking about curiosity, warns the reader that through extroversion, we could go beyond Dinah and Eve to become imitators of Satan (*immo ipsius Satanæ imitatorem te dixerim*) (#29). Despising the brethren, the abbot and God, and thereby cutting himself off from them, the proud monk has fulfilled this prophecy, this dire prophecy. The whole beautiful world of interpersonal communion, the real Christian world, the real monastic world, has disappeared for him.

Conference 10

Pride and the Collapse of Our Humanity

We have been talking about pride, the whole evolution of pride and its consequences, and we have seen how Saint Bernard really attributes two origins to it. One is a kind of negligence, a negligence of that first commandment of God which is to dwell in our heart through contemplation and self-awareness. And the other is related to it, it is an intolerance of our own hearts. We cannot bear to live with our inner poverty. On the first day I quoted three similes that Bernard gives; he says that for the proud person to live in his own heart is like living with dripping water, with a fireplace that is smoking, or with a wife who never shuts up. And so the person can't take it and flees out of himself into extroversion, which Saint Bernard calls curiosity. We saw the development of that curiosity and how it seems so mild in the beginning but is terrible in its conclusion, especially because it destroys relationships. Remember, we saw the false relationship it creates with the brethren, and then the inability to accept the ongoing relationship with the abbot to such an extent that Saint Bernard says, "When you've reached the tenth degree of pride you can't really stay in the monastery anymore, it becomes impossible. For you it is hell and for the community it is also, so you have to go." Ultimately it destroys your relationship with God as well, as it becomes contempt for God and his commandments.

This morning, we are going to look at the same phenomenon but under a different angle: pride as the collapse of our humanity. As Christians our authentic humanity is established on a triple foundation: the revealed divine law (or you could think of it as the natural law, as we'll see), the magisterium of the Church, and the inner voice of our own conscience. That's what makes us human, christianly speaking—that we live directed by the divine law, the teaching of the Church, and the inner voice of our own conscience. To persevere in this humanity requires humility; to keep each of these foundations firm requires the obedience of faith. In the second half of the treatise that we are studying, Saint Bernard shows us not only how pride destroys relationships (Conference 9) but also how it eats away at our specific human identity.

The finest and most delicate of these foundations is the voice of conscience, this constantly being led by the Holy Spirit, what I call the little voice. So I will throw in another of my novitiate anecdotes. When I was a novice (I don't think it has stopped even now completely), I was a bookaholic, not only in reading books but in buying them and having them. I once tried to explain to Dom Augustine that the supreme moment of my relationship with the book is after I have bought it and am going home on the subway; it is still in the wrapping paper and I haven't opened it. He said, "That's crazy—you haven't read it." I said, "That's right." He said, "No that's wrong." I said, "No, that's right." He said, "Well how could it be right?" I said, "That's because until you have opened it, a book is infinite in what it might be able to offer you, but once you have started to read it is just a book." He said, "I still think it's crazy." And I said, "We are different." So when I went into the observership, I warned Father Joseph Chu Cong, "Beware. I am a bookaholic and I will be sure to ask permission to buy books, but don't let me." "Oh thank you very much for telling me." "You're welcome." So things were fairly quiet in the observership, but when I got into the postulancy I said to myself, "Let me give it a try." So I went to Father Joseph and said, "You know, they've just come out with a new translation of the Bible, the *New English Bible*, and they say that it is excellent. It is very literary and very accurate at the same time, and I think that would help me with my lectio. Do you think I could order a copy?" "Oh sure!" So we did. I was hoping that that would calm me—and it did, for a couple of weeks. "Father

Joseph, I got a letter from Dom Thomas Keating and he said that the very best book on the relationship between Christianity and Buddhism is called *Zen and the Bible*; it is a very good interpretation of gospel texts. I don't think we have it in the library, and even if we did it would be very useful for me to have a personal copy. Do you think I could order that through the librarian?" "Oh no, Father Bernard." "No? But how come, Father Joseph?" "Because you are a bookaholic." I said, "Oh, you remember." He said, "Of course I remember." I said, "Why did you let me order the first book?" He said, "I wanted to see how it worked." So there I was: Book, book, book, book, book, and book. And no way to get one. So I thought, "Okay, what could be a substitute?" It could be assembling them in my room, even from the library. It was not the same as buying them, but having them is still something. So here is the story about conscience. I went into the solarium, where the novices have their coffee break every morning, and there was a whole shelf of books: *Cities of the World*. There was a city I always wanted to visit but had never visited: Venice. So after the other novices left I went and took that book on Venice. I was going to take it to my room (that is all right as there is nothing in the *Constitutions* against that), when I heard a voice saying, "Put that book down." Who said that? Nobody. I thought, "I am taking this monastic life too seriously and I'm getting scrupulous. I will talk about it with the novice director next week." So I picked it up again and this time I heard, "I said, 'Put that book down.'" So I looked around again and there was still nobody there. So I said, "Well, maybe I need a novice director *and* a psychologist." That's a cocktail that has a punch to it. I picked it up again and once again I heard interiorly, "Bernard, this is the last time I'm going to tell you, 'Put that book down, and if you don't put it down I will never talk to you again.'" And then I knew things were serious, and that there is such a thing as the voice of conscience, and that the voice of conscience is what Cardinal Newman says it is: it is not just our own human voice but it is a dialog between God's voice and our human receptivity. And I knew that I was on the way to damaging that irretrievably, and that the Holy Spirit was serious. If you don't want to listen to the voice of your conscience, well don't, but then something awful happens: it stops talking. It can be silenced, at least to a great extent. Thanks be to God, I put the book down. Ever since then I have referred to the voice of conscience, to the Holy Spirit in the conscience, as "the Voice." That's the finest and most delicate of the foundations of our Christian humanity. The most delicate because we can shut it up, we can turn it off, and we can make it inaudible. One of the central functions of our conscience is to manifest to us the underlying intention of the act we are considering. Ever since Augustine, if not before, the theological tradition has affirmed the critical role of intentionality in human action, to such an extent that he said, with some justice, in his *Commentary on the First Letter of John* and in other places, that the intention defines the act. If you hit your child because he's done something awful, but it's out of love because you want to help him to get onto the right path, that act is a loving act. If you do it out of irritation or because you are personally offended, that same action is a sin. It is for this reason that Augustine could make what I consider his most famous "dare": "Love, and go ahead and do what you will." What he is saying is that when the intention is love, then the act becomes loving. You have to have a fairly delicate conscience to know what the intention really is.

In the sixth degree of pride, the monk purposely silences the awareness of his intention (*Quid intendat non attendit*) (#43). He doesn't pay attention to what he is intending because it is not favorable to his project of pride. Were he to pay attention to it, he would be forced to realize that what he is engaged in is a full-time attempt to fool others into believing in his sanctity by showing off his work (*operum ostentatione*). He suppresses the consciousness of his intention. "He purposely forgets it," says Saint Bernard. He forgets his intention (*obliviscitur intentionem*); he doesn't look at his acts to see where they're coming from. What he is doing is that instead of using intention as the key to what an action is, he makes opinion the key to what an action is. What other people say about his action, particularly when he can wheel and deal them into having the opinion he wants—*that's* what makes an act saintly. That will be the meaning of his action; instead of *intentio* it becomes *opinio.* He makes a decision that, rather than persisting in the hard and humbling work of self-knowledge, of self-awareness, he will once and for all judge himself in accordance with the praise that his actions elicit. And in doing this he has formed something, which for Saint Bernard is very important; *he has formed the thought of the heart.* Up until now pride could have been reversed with some measure of ease. But Saint Bernard says that there always comes a crucial moment in the passage from humility to pride when pride takes its seat within our hearts, in the *intimo cordis affectu.* This *affectus* takes stable possession of the heart and the content of this *affectus* is that we are better than everyone else. That's what the proud man has been working toward, and that is what he has convinced other people into believing. In several places in his writings, Saint Bernard speaks of the decisiveness of the moment when an *affectus* passes into the heart. It is a lengthy process, because the "heart" is what is deepest in us, and nothing is radically inserted there except at the cost of great desire, effort and time. Once it has been inserted, however, it is there to stay. We all have passing thoughts that are both divine and demonic but they fundamentally don't do a thing to us, because a passing thought does not become an *affectus* of the heart, except through a very long process. You really have to keep thinking it, and keeping that thinking going requires repeated choices—and all of that takes a long time. Thanks be to God, especially when it has to do with something like arrogance which is the sixth degree of pride. You can't become arrogant in the twinkling of an eye. That is a great blessing that it can't happen immediately—but it *can* happen eventually.

The proud man feels that he has gained immensely by this insertion. Because from now on, it is absolutely and unshakeably clear to him that he is better than all others. Remember, in the previous steps of pride there was insecurity. The person was trying to prove through his know-it-allness, through his extraordinariness, that he was better. But he wondered whether it was really true. And that's why he had to keep interrupting others when they were talking. He had to be the person who had the answer to all the questions, had to stay up later before the Blessed

Sacrament, even if it meant he slept through Vigils, had to eat less in public even if he gorged himself in private. All of these things were ways of trying to convince himself that he was better by convincing others. But now the mirror (the voice of other people) constantly says what he wants to hear. "You're it." In the novitiate I had a dream when the whole community circled my bed and one after another bowed and said, "We love you, we love you." That was a prevision of the sixth degree of pride. I enjoyed that dream tremendously. It was a Joseph dream, a dream of grandiosity, and someone should've thrown me into a well. It seems like there's been a tremendous gain through this, because now it is not in question anymore—I am better than others. I am because everybody's saying it, and that echoes in me now without any inner uncertainty. In truth, however, the monk has sacrificed precisely that instrument by which he could have become genuinely good. Holiness can only happen through the conscience, the commandments of God, the magisterium of the Church. We need them to become holy, but the holy person is the person constantly receptive to the inner movement of the Spirit. Without that, you can't have union of spirit. The first step to *unio spiritus,* which we Cistercians consider the apex of sanctity, is responsiveness to the motions of the Holy Spirit, and if you sell that for the sake of hearing people tell you that you're better than everybody else, if others quash that knowledge that you are really after, and you base your opinion of yourself on what other people are saying, and assume that your deeds are terrific because everyone's telling you that, you can never really become holy, unless that is reversed. Having lost your conscience you can never again have the "testimony of a good conscience" which Saint Bernard, citing Saint Paul, designates as our "glory." Instead, such a person can only hear a perpetual public announcement, "You're holier than all others, you're holier than all others," an announcement that from now on is incapable of being modulated or modified by reality. Instead of sensitivity to what is going on within him, the proud man lives with a single self-imposed conviction. And this conviction is highly dangerous because of its immobility. Henceforth whatever he does, it will be right. That is why in the eighth degree of pride, such a person defends his errors so tenaciously. In the final analysis his acts *cannot* be wrong, because they are his, and he devoutly believes himself to be better than others. Such a person can't be corrected. There is nothing to correct. So there has been a real destruction within this person when he reaches the sixth degree of pride which is arrogance. When it becomes a permanent thought of the heart, based on public opinion but assumed into the heart, the lie has been taken into the heart that I am holier than all others. And the conscience becomes nonfunctional—and it's our own fault. That's how we wanted it.

The second foundation of our humanity is more solid and less easily removed. It is the authority of the Church, present, in this case, in the pastoral ministry of the abbot. We know that outside the context of spiritual direction, this authority does not normally direct itself to the inward intention of acts, but to the acts themselves. The abbot watches over the common life of the brethren, fosters those actions and attitudes that upbuild it, and corrects those that diminish it. His guide in this is obviously the Rule of Saint Benedict, beginning with the Instruments of Good Works and continuing with all the moral, legislative and normative elements in the Rule. In other words, the abbot's authority aims at maintaining the monastery as a school of the Lord's service. In Gethsemani we had, along with the conferences on Gilbert of Hoyland, an open meeting. Ask anything! The very last question came from Father Elias. "What's your definition, in a phrase, of a monastery?" he said. "Today many people say it's a family, but for me family is what you come from." I said, "You do live in two families, the one you come from and the one you build. But I am not sure either if that's the right phrase." So my mind whirled around—the bell had already rung for Vespers—and I said, "I don't think you can do better than what Saint Benedict says in the prologue. The monastery is a school of the Lord's service, *dominici schola servitii*. It is a school of learning of how to serve the Lord and how to serve as the Lord served and how to serve in a lordly way. All of those things are contained in that Latin phrase." It's very rich, and because of the genitives it can mean many different things: the school of the Lord's service can mean to learn how to serve the Lord, to learn how to be a servant as the Lord was servant, or to learn to serve in such a way that is a lordly service. Saint Benedict was clearly familiar with that famous ancient collect, "To serve him is to reign." As I see it, that is what the abbatial authority aims at, keeping the monastery as a school of the Lord's service in all those three senses. But it is exactly this authority that the proud monk rejects in the tenth degree of pride, which is rebellion.

The proud monk will not allow his acts to be "regulated," to be submitted to scrutiny and evaluation by any other person than himself. What he is rebelling against at this point is not the particular content of one or another monastic precept. It is not that he disagrees on the abbot's teaching on such and such a point. It is against the right of the Church, or in this particular case, the abbot, to govern and correct his actions. Why should another human person presume to assert himself over my behavior and to demand a public confession of guilt, a penance and an avoidance of this behavior in the future? Why should there be, in the broader sense, a magisterium? Why should there be someone who is my teacher? I tell the novices that when they come into Novo Mundo one of the hardest things to get used to is that you will be a disciple for the rest of your life. Monastic life is permanent discipleship—for the superior as well, in a different way, but just as deep I believe—but that's it, you are never going to be without a master, and the moment when you feel you would like to be is probably the moment when you most need it. I don't know if you know the Zen story—this, too, comes from Father Joseph Chu Cong—about a disciple who had spent ten years with his master, and the master very cleverly decided to have the celebration *before* conferring on the disciple the title of master. The party was held one day before, and the master said, "This is your last opportunity to be a disciple, so you will serve the tea at the banquet and bow before each person in humility because it's your last day as disciple. Tomorrow *you* are the master." So the disciple went around and presented the tea to each person, bowing before him, and finally came to the master, and as he bowed to give the cup of tea to the master, the master slapped him. The monk blushed out of humiliated pride and the master said, "Oh well. Let's give it another ten years." It's an interesting parable and very helpful for us. It is a way of reconciling ourselves with the truth that, not only will we always be a disciple, but we'll always *need* to be a disciple, to be disciplined; because I think we can imagine our face getting red too, if we were at that glorification banquet. I will tell you a Zen tale that made that story true for me. I was prior at Spencer for one year, and during that year Dom Augustine turned sixty. He was leaving for a month's retreat on his birthday, after ten years of being superior. So I said to the cooks, "Let's have champagne because he's sixty and has been ten years a superior." He is a very beautiful person. Father Francis Michael can testify to that—I admire him greatly—but he's also a shy person, and shyness reacts in different ways to different circumstances. So the meal started, and he knew nothing about it. We were able to keep it as a surprise. Two minutes into the meal I rang the bell, which made him look at me, because it was not up to me to ring the bell; it was up to him to ring the bell. The doors of the refectory opened and I think it was Brother Jude, who was cook, who came down the center aisle with a cart with eighty glasses of champagne. And I got up and read a poem in his honor for his anniversary, and he got up and said, "That poem is the most sentimental thing I have ever heard." For me that was the monastic glorification banquet. There I was in front of eighty people, the prior, and he was about to leave for a month, and I would be the head authority of the community, and the ground, I felt, had just been cut out from under me. But I remembered the anecdote and I said, "Ten more years." At least the master always knows the way.

To be a monk or nun is to accept to be a disciple for the rest of your life. You need it. The blush or the sadness or the shrivelling inside means that humility has still not been fully realized within you. This is much, much worse for the person in the tenth degree of pride who simply rejects in principle the idea of being taught, of having a teacher who doesn't simply spout doctrine but who has the hands-on relationship of saying, "Listen: This, this and this have to change."

Once again, the proud monk's impression is that he has gained something by descending one more step on the ladder of pride. What has he gained? He has gained what Saint Bernard calls the *libertas peccandi*, the right to sin. It is now an acquired right. The right to be the only judge and ruler, humanly speaking, of his own actions, the right to do well or the right to sin as he pleases. No one is going to say that I can or cannot do this. I have the freedom to sin and that belongs to me. The freedom to sin is the analog in action to the knowledge of evil. What Adam and Eve gained in the way of consciousness, that's what this monk gains in the realm of doing. I'm free to do good and I'm free to do evil. I think we have all wrestled with Saint Augustine's definition of liberty, "Liberty is the ability to always do the good." Saint Bernard is completely in line with Augustine. For both of them, whenever you do evil, you are acting out of a diminished liberty. True liberty is when you are able and desirous and always actually doing the good. So once again this poor monk thinks he has gained something immense, but actually he has lost another indispensable bulwark of his humanity. Cassian says in his Third Conference that we have to find a counterweight to this tendency, that our liberty has to move away from a falsely conceived autonomy, and that one of the best counterweights is to live under the authority of an abbot and a rule. That is one of the chief reasons to do it, because you recognize that your liberty, in order to be true liberty, needs to be lifted up and rectified again and again, and that embracing communal living under a superior does elevate your liberty and keep it from a downward keel. It's a *contrapeso*. In the abbot there is a master who can effectively restrain the negative inclination of one's actions. Interestingly, the Jewish tradition has this also. They speak of what they call the *yetzer ha ra'a* which is the tendency toward evil. It's their phrase for concupiscence. They also assert that everyone has this tendency toward the good, but it doesn't exist in isolation. Both of the two urges are always at work in the person, which calls for continual vigilance. That's what we always have to be on the lookout for, this tendency of the evil inclination to assert itself. In the authority of the abbot there is someone to restrain the negative inclination and gradually alter this inclination so that it spontaneously tends to the good (twelfth degree of humility), so that it becomes second nature for the monk to want to do the good. Saint Bernard says that this monk in the tenth degree of pride has "lost his fear of the abbot" (*iam . . . abbatem non timet*) (#50). This fear should have been lived out until it fulfilled its function of producing a *conversio morum*. William of Saint Thierry says in his tripartite developmental scheme of the animal man, the rational man and the spiritual man that you know you have come to the end of your animal man stage when your instinctive inclination is to the good. And that it is your habitual inclination. It doesn't mean that the other inclination doesn't exist anymore, but now instead of there being a spontaneous decline there is a spontaneous ascent. That's what the abbot is for, that's what the Church is for, and that's what the magisterium is for: to change our appetite so that we delight in the good. That's what the monk has lost in the tenth degree of pride, the help of a teacher in the transformation of the inclination, as well as a guide to action. Now the only remaining foundation of humanity for this monk is the divinely revealed law.

By divinely revealed law, I mean God's commandments, both as written law and as internal assimilation of that written law— the universal precepts given at Sinai, now present and active in the human heart. They have been placed there by God, according to Saint Thomas and other theologians, as the most basic orientation and guarantee of our humanity, the essential tenets of the moral law. By the way, Father Francis Michael, I would like to know where those pencils that have the Ten Commandments come from. In the pencil box over there on the table is a pencil that says, "Thou shalt not kill." And another which says, "Thou shalt not covet thy neighbor's wife." And another pencil that says, "Thou shalt not steal." What is written on those pencils does not depend on our sensitivity to the Holy Spirit. You don't have to be a saint to have the content of those pencils within you, and you don't have to have an abbot to have the Ten Commandments inside you. The whole Catholic and Orthodox tradition says that the content of those teachings, those ten words, as the Jews say, are engraved within you. The Jewish tradition says that when they were engraved on the tablets of Sinai they were engraved on the tablets of the heart by the finger of God. They don't depend on our delicate conscience or on the moral authority of any institution to which we belong, whether monastic community, church or civil society. Intuitively we understand that they are written by the finger of God and that our life as human beings consists in obeying them. That is the fundamental work of our reason: to constantly perceive them and to convince us of their validity.

However, inside the human person there exists not only reason but also concupiscence. The power of this concupiscence had been diminished by living under the authority of the Rule and the abbot, and the workings of the inner conscience had made the monk capable of identifying and combating its first movement. But little by little these helps have been rejected by the proud monk, and it turns out that *ratio* in its "unsupported" state is no match for the onslaught of concupiscence. Concupiscence, once disciplined, but now let loose again, is like an enormous ocean wave that overwhelms us, Saint Bernard says, like a great whirlpool (*carnalium desideriorum voragine absorptus*) (#51). Once pent up and newly released, it is almost unthinkable that it can be subjected to control a second time. The only force great enough to dominate it would be a divine intervention in the form of punishment, a salvific anticipation of the final judgment that would still leave time to repent. But God does not respond to this dare: "Punish me, and I'll obey you again." Instead, he intervenes by *not* punishing now, showing the dreadful aspect of his patience (*terribili iudicio Dei prima flagitia impunitas sequitur*) (#51). Every time you are about to make a smart aleck remark and don't, why don't you—especially when it would be so funny? You don't because the workings of your conscience tell you that the possible hurt it could cause another person is much more important and morally significant than any guffaw that you might get out of the audience, so you don't say it. Many, many, many times concupiscence makes a possibility arise and yet your first reaction is, "No." Let me put a chart on the board that comes from Saint Bernard's commentary *On the Song of Songs*. Saint Bernard wants to know how people get caught in the passions, in the classical sense of the word, and he says this is how it happens; he makes a list of five stages. The first is simply that your concupiscence is always stirring up possibilities, possible pleasures, possible satisfactions, possible attractions; the thought comes into your head. You can say no to that if your conscience is delicate enough to realize that that's going on, and if your reason is clear enough to see it and your will is strong enough to say "thank you, but no." Remember how Saint Augustine said it is all right to look at a beautiful woman once because it just happens. But if you turn around and look at her a second time it moves quickly toward desire—and that's true not just for a beautiful woman, it is true for anything that the concupiscence has stirred up. If you cut it off then and there you are free. If you let it swirl around inside you, very quickly it attracts the will—and the will is wonderful at convincing the reason that it's right. (If you want to read the most brilliant text of Saint Bernard on that, see his long *Sermon on Conversion to Clerics*. Here the whole "inner family"—reason, will and motions of concupiscence—ends up living a confusion of roles, where the governing place of the reason is taken over by the will, and the will in turn is dominated by the multiple stirrings of desire). Let's say you haven't said "no" to this movement of concupiscence, and now you experience a desire. You can still say "no," but it is not as easy as it would have been before, or you can give in and say "yes." This is a sin, a sinful act. You have given in to a sinful prompting of the concupiscence, you have let desire exercise its pressure and you've done it. You go to confession, or if it's not something so serious you simply go to God and that's that. But as we know it is not that. The next day or a couple of days later, like the story about the bookaholic, the concupiscence comes back; "Gee, it would be fun to do it again." This time even though it starts out just on the level of thought it is much harder to cut, because the attraction has been strengthened by having done it. So it's much easier to slide to desire and a certain fatalism and you think there is no use resisting it because I did it yesterday and it is more than 90 percent likely that I am going to do it today. So you do it, and the act becomes a habitual act. Saint Bernard says you still have your freedom, because you can never not have your freedom. But a few days later there it is again, and this time, because it's a habit, the movement is much quicker down all of these steps, and finally it becomes a passion. A passion means it is almost true to say you can't help yourself. It is so rooted in you that that is how you are, that is what you do, and there is a wistful yearning that it could be different, but everything in you moves you to do it again and again and again, and be imprisoned by it. Saint Bernard says this can be undone—for him this is one of the rationales of monastic life—but that it's not easy. Saint Bernard says that our destiny as human persons is to end up in either *pure action* or *pure passion*. I think that's beautiful. What does that mean? If we end up in *pure action* it will mean that in heaven, even the constant joy and the beatitude that God gives us will not be experienced passively, but actively. Every moment of loving and knowing God for all eternity will be a human activity. We will be pure correspondence and collaboration with the beatific vision, and we will be *doing* it—for Saint Bernard we will be as much *doing* the beatific vision as enjoying the beatific vision. Enjoy doesn't mean just sit back and enjoy, that is not Saint Bernard's meaning of enjoy; to enjoy is *do* and to enjoy. We will become either pure action or pure passion. In hell, which for Saint Bernard is a real possibility, even our maliciousness, our hatred of God, our remorse will be things *inflicted* on us. They will be sufferings, rather than our own actions. The sadness of hell or the loss of God in hell, the lack of communion in hell, even if it does provoke in us hatred and malice —something in us will always regret that, and something in us will always know that we didn't choose it. It was chosen. To be in Hell is to submit to the consequences of having always passively submitted to our impulses. So we are destined to become pure action or pure passion. Saint Bernard's question is, "How free can you become from this cycle?" He says you can never get to zero. But what would zero mean? It would mean that there is no concupiscence. That you never experience a desire that goes against the will of God. That every divine inspiration meets with perfect collaboration, and nothing else ever comes up on the screen except what God wills. He uses Saint Paul to justify his teaching that concupiscence will persist until the end of our life. My novices are not satisfied with that. They say no, that's negative Augustinianism. What I want to say to them is: wait and you will see. I personally would be extremely happy if I could always remain there. Remaining there means that sometimes there passes through your brain the possibility of committing an imperfection or a sin, but because of your love of God and your habits and the transformation of the monastic *conversatio*, it never gets beyond that. What wouldn't I give to be there, and I think Saint Bernard is absolutely right. For this life, that is it! The Brazilians don't give up their aspirations easily, however. I have a young solemnly professed who when he was a novice heard about pure prayer as Evagrius defines it. He said to me, "Father Bernardo, by thirty I am going to have attained pure prayer." I said, "Who told you?" He said, "I am." I said, "How do you know?" He said, "Because I want it." I said, "Yeah, what else?" He said, "I am going to give everything I have to get there."

For a third time, the monk may feel he has gained something: freedom from the lordship of God. Saint Bernard shows us exactly what freedom from God's lordship consists in: the degradation of being a human beast. The category of right and wrong exists no longer; the only category is attraction, pleasure (*Libitis pro licitis utitur*) (#51). In this context, self-restraint is impracticable; worse than that, it is unthinkable. Everything depends on instinct; the person (if he still is one) pounces on whatever comes to mind, to mouth, to hand.

Without conscience, without the authority of the Church, without God's law, man becomes a monster. Look at him as Saint Bernard presents him: "He puts no brake on his experience of the forbidden, neither in considering forbidden things, carrying them out or searching out new possibilities. Whatever crime comes into his head, he meditates on it; whatever foulness comes into his mouth, he speaks it; whatever evil deed offers itself to his hand, he performs it. His will is evil; his words are empty; his deeds are detestable" (*Iam ab illicitis cogitandis, patrandis, investigandis animus, manus vel pedes non prohibentur; sed quidquid in*

cor, in buccam, ad manum venerit, machinatur, garrit, et operatur,
malevolus, vaniloquus, facinorosus) (# 51).

How humbly grateful we should be for these three foundations
of our humanity; how careful to build on them; how fearful of
losing them!

Conference 11

The Creator of Pride

Remember we said there were two icons to be found in the midst of our conferences, one of Christ as Extreme Humility and one of Lucifer (if you can say icon about Lucifer) as pure pride.

If we are at all "philanthropical," if we have any love for mankind, we will look outside of humanity for the source of that terribly self-destructive pride we contemplated in the last conference. Evagrius says we sin by concupiscence. Human beings sin basically by desire. It is the fallen angels who sin by violence. Our sins are more a wanting, a continual wanting. Real hatred as the basis of sin is more demonic than it is human. And Maximus the Confessor says something similar, that human beings sin by negligence. The hostility and hatred that overpower them enters into them through their lack of watchfulness, but they are not the origin of it. If a human being does hate, it is because he has been overpowered by the demons. For us to hate another human being would be like hating your own flesh and as Saint Paul says, "No one hates his own flesh." So when that hostility and hatred get into us they have a source that is not ourselves. Talking about the sin of Eve, Saint Bernard says, "You who were intent on something other than you should have been, the demon secretly slipped into your heart, speaking to you in a flattering way" (*Te enim intenta ad aliud, latenter interim in cor tuum serpens illabitur, blande alloquitur*) (#30). Writing in the same monastic tradition as Maximus, Saint Bernard asserts that pride, both in its first beginnings and in its full-blown form, results from the presence and "inspiration" of the evil one, initially accepted through curiosity. Lucifer is a purely spiritual creature, and as such is capable of making incessant interior "suggestions" that more and more firmly establish his dominion over the proud. In the fourth or fifth sermon *On the Song of Songs*, Bernard says that God is the only being who can speak in our hearts, who can inspire us, without our being aware of it. He is so interior to us as our Creator, as God, that he can subtly and imperceptibly inspire us to act for the good imagining that the idea came from us, whereas it really came from him. We think of those situation comedies on TV when an employee is in trouble with the boss, and the boss is in trouble with the business, and the wife of the employee comes up with the necessary solution but is savvy enough to recognize that the boss has to think that the great idea was his. So she successfully maneuvres things in that direction, and in the end, everything turns out well. "Wow, what a terrific idea I had." The employee and his wife know he didn't have it, but the employee keeps his job, the boss keeps his self-esteem and the wife keeps her secret. That's how it is between us and God: he is always inspiring us toward a good, but his way of acting is so interior, so pure, and so delicate that we don't perceive the divine inspirations. Not only that. The ability of God to act imperceptibly in us has to do with the fact that ontologically we are so related. As Saint Augustine says, "He is more inward to us than we are to ourselves." Now, thanks be to God, Saint Bernard would say, the devils can't do that. There is no other being except God who can act upon us in a totally impalpable way. The most that the demons can do, and what they do do, is to constantly make interior suggestions. That's the word Saint Bernard uses. Suggestions. But as Athanasius says in his *Life of Anthony*, those suggestions by a person who is seeking God will be felt as a kind of shock, as something like a disharmony, because they are not in accord with our habitual way of thinking. I do not know if you know of the comparison of Saint Ignatius of Loyola. He says that when a person seeking to live a holy life is visited by a demonic suggestion, it will feel like a drop of water falling on a stone. It will be a shock, whereas for a person who habitually lives in evil, a demonic suggestion will feel like a drop of water falling onto a sponge. No sound at all, no conflict at all—and the inverse is true of divine grace. For a person who is living the life of grace, these divine inspirations will feel exactly as if his own heart was speaking. A person living habitually in sin will experience divine grace as water on a stone. "What, stop stealing? Where did that come from? Crazy idea! I'm going to be careful about my diet from now on." Remember Scrooge, he thought that it was an undigested bit of beef that made him see the good spirit that came to visit him, because he wasn't living a good life, and so the good inspiration of God felt to him like the movements of an intruder. So Lucifer can only make suggestions, but he is very persistent about them. Like every human person, the proud man is essentially receptivity, and if he is not indwelt by the love and wisdom of God, the evil spirit will take advantage of this "vacuum" and fill the his heart with his own demonic *affectus:* "When the devil sees that in the heart of the proud there is no ray of wisdom that is shining, there is no fire of love that is burning, he takes that as a vacuum and he makes his house there and exerts his dominion there" (*Quos utique . . . prævidens nullo quidem sapientiæ radio coruscantes, nullo spiritu amoris ferventes, velut vacuum repereris locum affectasti super illos dominium) (#36). It is the parable of the seven demons taking possession of the empty house (Luke 11:24-26).

What is the aim of Lucifer's pride and what are the attitudes that characterize it? Like all pride, it is love of one's own specialness: *amor propriæ excellentiæ.* That is a definition that Saint Bernard never veers away from. In Lucifer's case, his "peer group" is formed by his fellow angels, the seraphim and the cherubim, and he seeks to surpass them by making the only upward move possible: to turn himself into a second God. There is a verse from Isaiah that is always used by the Fathers to describe the intentions of Lucifer: "I will be like the Most High": *Ero similis Altissimo* (Is 14:14, Vulg). Whereas all the angelic hosts stand in adoration of the one God, Lucifer wants to sit at God's side, to be enthroned along with God and be the object of heaven's veneration.

Saint Bernard says that Lucifer's pride is *gratuitous* and *absurd.* It is gratuitous because he was the most gifted and glorious of all creatures by nature. He was the star of the morning. According to tradition he was the most beautiful and intelligent of all the angelic hosts. Among the created spirits, there was not his equal. So what more could you want? And yet he did want more. It's gratuitous because he had it all and was not satisfied, and it is absurd because ultimately it is impossible. The Creator of all established him in his proper place. Like the rest of us, Lucifer could either "stand" in his identity or "fall" from it, but he could not transcend it. So Saint Bernard, who has a dialogue with Eve and with Dinah, also has a dialogue with the devil: "Stand in yourself lest you fall from yourself if you walk in great things and things beyond yourself" (*Sta in te, ne cadas a te, si ambulas in magnis et in mirabilibus super te) (#31)*. Before mocking him too much, however, we might like to ask if we do not likewise participate in the gratuity and absurdity of his pride, through ingratitude for the plenitude we have received, and doomed attempts to be other persons than the ones we have been made. There is a young priest in my community who loves attention (he says so himself), and from time to time he comes to me and says, "Father Bernardo, you give me everything, but I want more." It's a very interesting contradiction in which there is a fair amount of self-knowledge. He knows that everything I have to give him, I give him, and he is glad about that. But he wants more. So we too participate in the gratuity and absurdity of pride.

This overweening pride of Lucifer expresses itself in the two interwoven attitudes of *malice (malitia)* and *cunning (astutia)*. Lucifer is malicious in his ingratitude. Not only is he passively ungrateful, failing to give thanks to him who raised him out of nothing to angelic dignity; he is actively ungrateful, seeking to disturb the celestial harmony that God has established (*status æternitatis)*, that beautiful harmony which rules all of heaven. He wants to disrupt it by raising himself out of his place and putting himself in God's place. And he wishes to injure God by attempting to impose himself as a second God, although he knows that this is neither good, nor in conformity to the divine will, and that it will be a constant grief to God: "Against God's will, you hope and aspire to become equal to him, though as a consequence God should ever have to behold what grieves him" (*altissimo Domino, licet invito, desideras et speras æquari, quatenus semper videat quod doleat* (#33). "So what?" says Lucifer.

I don't know if you remember the television show "Andy's Gang." It was a TV show for children on Saturday and it had a character that was called Froggy. At some point in the program Froggy would appear, and Froggy was malice incarnate. He loved to do things just to hurt people and grieve them. Every week there was Andy the moderator, Froggy and a "special guest star." The incident that I remember is one in which the guest star was a French chef and he was giving a lesson about how to make a soufflé. Froggy is reading the recipe to the chef, who follows Froggy's instructions step by step. "And you take six eggs." "I take six eggs" (He takes them). "And you crack them." "And I crack them." (He cracks them.) "And then you pour them over your head." "I pour them over my head." And the French chef pours them over his head and there they are. "Ha, ha, ha, I did it, I did it," says Froggy. Of course, this appeals to the demon in every one of the children watching the show. Froggy was my great hero. I do not know if I have given him up yet. So the devil is malicious.

No one is better spiritually informed than Lucifer, and he should be the first to realize that his ambition is doomed. How is he going to succeed in making himself God? How is this going to work? Is he going to force his way into being God, and then have God just sit back and take it as something that cannot be acted against, as a fait accompli? Lucifer however does not plan to attain his objective through mere power, but through power and trickery (*astutia*). His plan is to use God against God. And evidently all through this analysis of Lucifer, Saint Bernard is talking about the worst that pride could bring about in us. Each time you look at the moves Lucifer makes you have to ask yourself, "Do I fit in here also?" As Lucifer sees it, God's will and God's power are conditioned by God's goodness. God cannot exercise his power in a form contrary to his goodness, without being deprived of his goodness. "Granted," says Lucifer, "that God *would* and *could* act against my scheme and overturn me in a moment." But God knows that he *should* not act in this way. It would be an unthinkable *malum divinum*, it would be evil on the part of the divine to avenge himself on Lucifer, because God is good, because God is forgiving, God is benevolent, God is mercy. So God must simply accept the affront. God is rendered helpless by his own benevolence. For Lucifer, God's sweetness (*dulcedo*) turns God into a victim. That's how Lucifer sees the way it is going to play itself out. Lucifer is going to host a rebellion, set up a rebellion, and they're all going to march against God and God is going to sit back and take it, because to overwhelm Lucifer would mean to use violence. It would mean to have to hurt someone, to hurt his own creatures, and God who is love would never do anything to hurt his own creatures. So God is chained by his own gentleness, by his own mercy, by his own being a good guy, and Lucifer is going to march in and set up his throne—God is helpless. The question is if we don't sometimes think and act in that way ourselves.

Saint Bernard marvels at the intensity of malice that exists in the apostate seraph. He concedes a certain tragic aesthetic beauty to the notion of God that Lucifer has fashioned: a God so good, so committed to his creatures, that rather than vindicate himself, he willingly suffers an eternity of offense. "Yet," says Bernard, "should not such a notion of God serve as an irresistible stimulus to love him and devote oneself to him?" He says, "Lucifer, let's pretend that God is the way you propose him, that he is one hundred percent mercy and nothing else, that he has renounced his omnipotence and submitted it absolutely to his goodness and pardoning. Now shouldn't that win your heart? Shouldn't that be the most persuasive motivation for giving up this plan of rebellion? If you're not going to adore the God who is power, won't you be moved to adore the God who is so completely self-sacrificing love that he gives up the absoluteness of his divinity in order not to hurt you?" Saint Bernard writes, "Certainly Lucifer, if this is how you really see him, you act all the more wickedly if this does not bring you to love him" (*Certe si talis est qualem putas, tanto nequius agis, si non amas* (#33). Amazingly, this concept of God which Lucifer has formed for himself does not convert him; instead it assures him that God may be safely dealt with as a pawn. Remember the eleventh and twelfth degrees of pride when the human person does the same thing? God doesn't punish. "The fool has said in his heart, there is no God." I think "there is no God" in the context of the psalms doesn't mean that God doesn't exist. That's not so interesting. It means God doesn't act, it means God is not a presence of justice in this world. He is not the guardian of deepest values and not the one who shows that they are stable in human existence. So now Lucifer feels safe, and instead of this new notion making him love God, it makes him despise God. (One thinks inevitably of the mockery of shorn Samson, and even more of the mockery of our Lord in his passion.) Lucifer presumes, and here is the root of all presumption, that God's mercy is the one efficacious arm that exists against God's justice. He has found the only thing that could be used against God, and it is in God himself. God is helpless against his own mercy. What could not be found in any human arsenal, demonic cunning, this *astutia*, has been found in God's stockpile.

The proud man at the end of his downward journey (twelfth degree), the proud monk, asserts that God does not punish. The reason does not interest him; the important thing is that the connection between sin and punishment has been severed. Lucifer asserts that in order to be faithful to his own nature, God *cannot* punish. He has raised the experience of the proud monk to the level of a theological tenet. I think there are theologians out there who are saying this today: if God is mercy, God cannot punish. God's mercy means that his justice has been swallowed up, and he renounces it, and has eternally renounced it. Lucifer has made God into a machine, and in the divine goodness he has found the lever with which to control him. Ultimately Lucifer's astuteness is foolishness. "Blinded by his pride," says Saint Bernard, "he has worked out in his head a vision of God that will keep God from interfering with his plan." The one thing that Lucifer did not take into account is that maybe God is not as he thinks he is. Remember that the only thing worse than *voluntas propria* is *arbitrium proprium,* where you think that whatever you think is true because you thought it. Lucifer was unable to question the portrait that he painted of God. If he painted it, that's how it is. But God is not Lucifer's vision of God—as he is not our vision of God. God is himself. God is supremely free, supremely good, supremely just, and his attributes do not cancel each other out. Rather, they compenetrate each other. That means that every divine act is at one and the same time an expression of liberty, justice and goodness. Every time God acts, in that single act are liberty, justice and goodness. They don't cancel each other out and don't alternate. They are always fully present. In the final analysis it *is* an act of divine goodness for God to assert his unique sovereignty. It is fidelity to the supreme good, and it is the defense of the goodness of the order he has created, order by means of which he communicates being, life, wisdom and love to his creatures and preserves them in his peace. Life is hard enough for us with Lucifer in hell; what would it be like if he were co-God in heaven? So it is an act of tremendous goodness that God makes Lucifer incapable of realizing his plan. In Brazil there is a joke about the captain of a cruise ship. This captain is a martinet. He treats everybody with disdain, especially the crew. He just takes advantage of every situation to scream at, humiliate and punish the crew and the passengers. But he's at Mass every day and takes Communion. The priest sees he is giving Communion to the captain the first day, but he does not know what kind of a person he is. The second day he is a bit wiser, he has witnessed a couple of things, and is a little surprised that the captain is there taking Communion. Between the second and the third day he witnesses a scandal. He sees the captain striking one of the officers, and he waits for the captain to come to confession. No confession! The next day there's the captain at Mass again and again he takes Communion. Finally, the priest goes to the captain and says, "Let me see if I'm looking at one person or two persons. You are the captain, right?" "Right." "You are the person that runs the ship, right?" "I run the ship." "And you're the person that mistreats everybody?" "Yes." "And yet every day there you are at Mass and you take Communion under both species." "Yes." The priest then says, "I don't understand how you can go to Communion." He said, "Father, if this is how I act when I go to Communion every day, imagine what I would be like if I didn't go to Communion every day!" If Lucifer makes our lives so troublesome chained up in hell, imagine how he would be if he were up there on the second throne. It is such a tremendous act of divine justice, and goodness and mercy that God does not let the devil's rebellion succeed.

The astuteness of pride is necessarily doomed wherever it exists, precisely because of God's justice. Not only does it end up humiliated, but ridiculed. Because God has an astuteness of his own, which even though inseparable from his mercy nevertheless fulfills his justice. Here is how it works: this is God's astuteness, and maybe the poet Milton copied it. Saint Bernard says that in punishing Lucifer, God perpetually holds open the possibility of pardon, should Lucifer repent. That's the divine mercy. "I want you to know the day you say you're sorry you have everything back again. All of your prerogatives will be yours." Yet he knows that Lucifer will never repent and will therefore never obtain pardon. Because in Lucifer's case, his attributes function in tragic opposition: his desire to be reinstated in his former glory is nullified by his inability to seek forgiveness (*temperans in vindicta sententiam, ut, si velis resipiscere, non neget veniam, secundum tamen duritiam tuam et cor impænitens, non possis velle, et ideo nec pœna carere*) (# 33). *Non possis velle*: Just as God cannot will evil, Lucifer is incapable of willing the good that would restore him to grace.

At the conclusion of this excursus, where he describes Lucifer's pride, Saint Bernard marvels one last time over this phenomenon. "What was it that you hoped to obtain by it?" he asks. "What was the purpose that drove you to your own destruction? In a word, it was the desire for power over others." Lucifer's pride is something that Augustine speaks about quite frequently: the desire to control others, the *libido dominandi*. It is very strong in the fallen personality. Those of you who have read *The Screwtape Letters*, and many of you have, know that C.S. Lewis describes the ultimate control that the devil desires to have over us as the act of devouring us. That is when the devil conquers us definitively, when we become his next meal. He lives off the lives of others. He himself is emptiness and thus the only way he keeps himself nourished is by devouring the lives and the creative goodness of creatures who let themselves go completely over to his side. This is how he will be like the Most High, he thinks: by ruling. But is this really how God identifies himself? For Lucifer, God is God because he controls, because he rules, because he has power. And of course, he does really does have power, he does order, but I don't believe that this is what makes God consider himself the Most High. It's simply another part of Lucifer's misunderstanding of God to affirm that he is the *Altissimus* because he holds the power *(regeres, per quod Altissimo similis esses)* (#36).

Saint Bernard wonders if perhaps Lucifer with his sharp-eyed spiritual intuition somehow understood the whole tragic story before it all happened. Maybe it is possible that he saw that it was going to come to this, but he accepted his condemnation and fall for the sake of being king of those who are destitute of God's wisdom and love, the more the better. Saint Bernard isn't sure and so he questions, "Yet can it be that Lucifer's pride deceived him to such a point"—and it is here that he is almost identical to Milton—"that he preferred to rule in misery than to serve in happiness?" *(cum tanta miseria cuperes principari, ut malles misere præesse quam feliciter subesse)* (# 36). "Can you be as insane as that," Bernard apostrophizes Lucifer. "Can you be as crazy as that, that you would desire to be a prince bound in such great misery, that you would prefer to dominate miserably than to serve happily?" The problem is that for Lucifer dominating *is* happiness. That's what he believes, and similarly, serving is sadness, so he can't really understand those phrases "to dominate miserably" or "to serve happily." Both of them are paradoxes that don't compute for him. In the end, Saint Bernard, being a humble man, finally affirms that Lucifer could not have been *that* power hungry. In other words, he could not have known that it would come to this. No one could be that foolish, to do something that would assuredly bring about the loss of eternal happiness. He says, "To that extent at least, he must have acted in ignorance—he could not have acted with full knowledge so totally against his own well-being." Those among us who have ever suffered the itch of the *libido dominandi* might be tempted to

give another answer. I think there is something in us, that sometimes the desire to lord it over others can be so strong that even if
it means being filled with misery, the attraction of pure power
would be enough to win us over.

*In response to a question about what might happen to a proud person
at the moment of meeting God:*

I don't have a difficulty with that idea if we understand that
our thought at the moment of encountering God isn't going to
be different than our thought before encountering God. It is the
idea of Saint Bernard that we are in the process of forming the
thoughts of our hearts which are very deep and permanent and
take a long time to form, and are almost impossible to unform.
So if the thought that has been formed throughout a lifetime is
a thought of being better than others, unable to live as a disciple
of anyone and intolerant of God's commandments, it is very hard
to imagine that at the moment of seeing God face to face we are
going to give him a big kiss. To say that is to assert a radical
discontinuity in the human person. Now we would like to think
that there is this beautiful, untouched spark of goodness that is
the real self that has never been affected negatively by that whole
life. That's where I can't agree. That says that our whole life as
we have lived it and thought it and decided it really does not
express who we are. There is this inner paradise that has never
been touched and that is who all of us are and when we see God
face to face, in the presence of that light, that paradise will blossom. I don't think that's so. I think like Gregory of Nyssa, whom
I quoted the other day, that we give birth to ourselves. This is the
immense responsibility that God has given us, and this is what
this last conference is about, and also some of these questions.
The immense responsibility that God has given us in collaboration with his grace to work out our eternal destiny. In his little
book *Credo* von Balthasar wrote meditations on the Creed for the
diocesan bulletin. (I would like to know if the typical parishioner
was able to understand those meditations. They are very brief,
none of them is more than four pages, but it took me hours and

hours and hours to really think my way through each of those meditations. You know what a church bulletin is like, the reflection is on the back page and you read it between the announcements. Von Balthasar must have had an immense confidence in the run-of-the-mill Swiss parishioner.) In one of those meditations he says, and this is very much in the tradition of *lectio*, that the last judgment will be an exegesis of our life as we have made it. We will see our life, really see it. We will see what we have known all along and know that we knew it, and we will simply read it out loud—and that will be the last judgment. Nothing more will be said. But I like that, because it refers to Christ's word in John's gospel, "I am not the one who judges." And yet it also says that there is a unity in our whole existence, and it is going someplace. Saint Thomas says at the very beginning of the second part of the *Summa*, "Man has an eternal destiny. It is the same for everyone. You can either get there or not get there." And that's the drama of human existence. It's one single eternal destiny that God holds out to us, but it is not a philosophical necessity that everybody gets there. You can either get there or not get there.

In response to a question about the Good Thief:

The "Good Thief" is badly named. His story is wonderful and it's a story that Saint Bernard would certainly be in agreement with, and I am too. That God through a powerful intervention can turn around an existence even at the last moment, that this does not lie outside the possibility of God's omnipotence. Saint Bernard says this too, but what the good thief cannot be taken as is a model for human living. Because the good thief is not an expression, he is not the archetype, of the situation of each of us. He's an incredible possibility of divine mercy and I think we should all identify with him to the extent that we will know that at the last judgment we need mercy to be saved. What he doesn't function as is a model for us, an example to be imitated: knowing about that story and using it as a lifetime basis for doing whatever I want, saying that I know at the end, I can say, "Lord, remember me when you enter into your kingdom," and that will do it all. Essentially that is the case of Lucifer. He felt that God would have to say to him. "I love you, I forgive you. I give you what you ask for." There is a whole tradition regarding the "thoughts of the heart"; I'd like to know more about it. I know Saint John of the Cross uses the term and I know Saint Bernard uses the term, and I know De Rancé uses the term. It seems to mean that there are a very small number of very deep convictions about reality at our core, and that these orient us constantly. And it is interesting that those whom I've identified with that tradition, the three that I mentioned, say that we are responsible for those thoughts. I think Saint Bernard would say that it is on the basis of them that we will be judged, because as I was saying when I was commenting on the von Balthasar book, deep, deep down we know what those thoughts are and we know if they're right or if they're wrong. I think I told this story about learning that I was a sinner when I was a novice in the Jesuits. That was the thought of the heart I had for twenty-four years, that I was not a sinner. A month before waking up to reality, there was a meeting of the whole province, and the provincial gave a beautiful homily on the fact that we as Jesuits are loved sinners. After the homily he wanted to know if there were any questions. And I in my deep humility—I had been a month or two in the order—had a question. "Why does it always have to be a loved sinner? Why can't it just be that we are God's loved creatures? Why do we always have to say we are loved sinners?" And the provincial said, "Because we *are* sinners, and we can either be loved sinners or not loved sinners, but you can't take the sinner part away." When he said that, I wasn't convinced. In God's mercy I went off to do the long retreat and was given the answer that showed me that the provincial knew what he was talking about. It would seem, and this is pure extrapolation at this point, that one of these deep, deep thoughts in the heart of the good thief was some kind of residual openness to the manifestation of God's mercy. But again, as I say, I wouldn't want to use it as a program for behavior. I think that would be terribly dangerous.

Conference 12

Limits, Consciousness, Responsibility

In the course of this treatise, Saint Bernard touches implicitly on a number of moral-ascetical issues that have importance for our living out of our monastic vocation. I would like to address three of them, trying to make them more explicit. They all have to do with the theme of personal responsibility.

The first issue has to do with the necessity of living in poverty of spirit. What is the responsibility of a monk who in the light of Truth has discovered his *vilitas*, has seen that up to now he has lived in a way that makes him blush for shame (*tales se videre cogunt, quales vel a se videri erubescunt*) (#18)? Saint Bernard answers in terms of the beatitudes. More or less hidden in paragraph 18 is a series of beatitudes that he must embrace one by one in order to pass from this first experience of truth to the second, mercy.

The monk who comes face to face with his "vileness" initially attempts to transform himself into a new person, all the while doubting his ability to accomplish this task on his own. Continuing to *mourn* over his past life and what he has become (*sese lugere*), he finds his only *consolation* in *hungering and thirsting for justice (amore veri esuriant et sitiant iustitiam)* (#18), demanding of himself complete satisfaction for his past misdeeds and whole-hearted amendment for the future. Yet his doubts prove true—try as he might, he remains a useless servant—and so he "flees from justice to mercy." In order, however, that *he may obtain mercy*, he himself begins to *show mercy to others*.

In a few closely packed lines, Bernard shows the intense personal struggle of the monk who has become "disillusioned" with his previous self-idealization. There is genuine *compunction,* heartfelt grief in the honest contemplation of a self who now totally displeases him. There is a generous effort at *conversion,* an attempt to make amends to God for the past *(satisfactio)* and live in accord with the divine will in the future *(emendatio).* There is the unvarnished recognition that after all "no man can pay the price for his own life" (Ps 48), and there is the humble acceptance that divine mercy is only for those who show human mercy. Every step of the process is marked by seriousness and the desire to please God, and this profound intention to become as God would have him be is what leads him step by step from humility to charity.

It is worth pointing out this process and underlining its significance, because there exists a tendency today to find a shortcut between humility and mercy. The novice seeking to faithfully carry out the requirements of the monastic life comes in touch with his defective inner attitudes, his passions, even his *vilitas.* Often enough, however, he finds his way too quickly to the divine mercy. There is no grieving, no striving, no suffering at the inability to carry out the divine will in its integrity, no agonized necessity to experience God's pardon and compassion. Instead, he immediately finds in the divine mercy an acceptance of himself just as he is, a dispensation from all further strenuous efforts at holiness and a guarantee that if he does not demand monastic *iustitia* from others, they will not have the right to demand it from him. This is an instrumentalization of the divine mercy, a diminished form of the presumption we saw in the previous conference. Only the monk who passes one by one through the beatitudes as Saint Bernard gives them and has the patience to experience each of them for as long as it lasts will arrive at the mercy that is the anointing of the Holy Spirit. If humility is not a first flower of the monastic life but already a solid sign of monastic maturity, how can it be expected that mercy/charity will realize itself in the beginner? All the more so as Saint Bernard himself weeps before the Lord in this treatise, saying that up to now he has not even reached the first heaven of humility (*Sed quid ego miser, superflua magis loquacitate quam spiritus vivaci-*

tate duos cælos superiores percurro, qui manibus pedibusque repens adhuc sub inferiore laboro?) (# 24).

The second issue deals with the persistence of moral responsibility in a person unconscious of the true nature of his attitudes and actions. Today we are very much inclined to believe that unawareness and subjective innocence are almost identical. Saint Bernard offers a different interpretation. We recall that the sixth step of pride is "arrogance" when the monk comes to believe with all his heart that he is holier than everyone else. Where has this conviction come from? Reading over the previous steps, we see that it is the consequence of many decisions, from the decision to not abide in oneself through vigilance to the decision to suppress the consciousness of the excellence of others in order to exalt one's own, and so on. These decisions, though taken under increasing psychological pressure (produced by the monk himself) were nevertheless *free* and the monk is responsible for the results. As we have said earlier in the course, the monk has thereby produced a "thought of the heart," a stable *affectus*, that henceforth will serve as the basis for future reflection and decision. Spiritual authors who treat these thoughts of the heart, such as John of the Cross and De Rancé, clearly affirm the individual's responsibility for the formation of this thought and for the actions he performs under its influence. Being proud to the point of having an unshakeable conviction of our superiority does not make us more innocent then we were when we were still working our way toward this belief.

The third issue is of ultimate moral responsibility, responsibility before the final judgment. Given that the treatise is a glorification of God's mercy shown to the humble, how can we doubt that this mercy will be universally efficacious? It is helpful in this instance to have just reflected over the final state of Lucifer. In him we contemplate a person to whom mercy is ceaselessly offered but who cannot benefit from it because his malice and the trickery of his mind have completely shut him up within himself. The proud man who despises God (*contemptus Dei*) is in an analogous situation. He is not touched by any person outside himself, not even by his true self, but only by his ever-more compulsive instincts and the state of mind produced by his constantly indulging them. Despising God, he does not merely challenge his justice while remaining open to his mercy. He declares God personally irrelevant in his life; whoever does not have the real power to interfere with his desires is irrelevant. He has become so *incurvatus in se* that God's mercy cannot find him.

That we have the right, the duty, the power and the inescapable obligation to choose our eternal spiritual destiny is a constant in the Church's theology. It is the gravest consequence of our liberty. We are capable of becoming such that no love, however salvific in itself, can save us. Saint Bernard does not counsel us to give up all hope for a living person who is in this state. Indeed he uses the examples of the efficacious intercession of Saint Martha, Saint Peter and the blessed Virgin in order to stir us to silently plead before the Lord for the conversion of such a brother or sister. But he does not hesitate to say that such a person, spiritually speaking, is already dead, buried and decomposing (see the comparison he makes between the final steps of pride and the sequence death-burial-decomposition: #55).

Humility or pride is man's most fundamental attitude before reality, and before the infinite reality who is God. As humility unites us with all other persons eventually making us capable of the *unio Spiritus* with God himself, pride excommunicates all other persons eventually making us uninterested in them and forgetful of their existence. That is why Saint Benedict gave us the steps of humility not to be studied but to be lived (*Benedictus non numerandos sed ascendendos proponit*) (#1). The past week has been a pause in our normal monastic *conversatio*, and we have spent it precisely in studying these steps. Tomorrow, God willing, I will offer some questions to help us reflect on our particular monasteries as schools of humility which, according to Saint Bernard, they must be if they are to become schools of charity and of contemplation (cf. General Chapter OCSO, 1996). As the week comes to an end, it is time once again to go climbing humility's steps in the day-to-day life of our communities.